SOCRATES
CAFÉ

3/11/01

For Mary,

Here's to the unending
joys of philosophical inquiry!

best wishes

C. P.

W · W · NORTON & COMPANY
NEW YORK · LONDON

SOCRATES CAFÉ

A Fresh Taste of Philosophy

CHRISTOPHER PHILLIPS

For information about permission to reproduce selections from
this book, write to Permissions, W. W. Norton & Company, Inc.,
500 Fifth Avenue, New York, NY 10110.

DISCLAIMER: To guard participants' privacy, all names and physical descriptions
have been changed; sometimes occupations and the locales at which dialogues
occurred have been changed. Participants portrayed in this book are occasionally
composites of those who took part in actual Socrates Café dialogues.

The text of this book is composed in Proforma
with the display set in Trade Gothic
Desktop composition by Molly Heron
Manufacturing by The Maple-Vail Book Manufacturing Group
Book design by Rubina Yeh

Library of Congress Cataloging-in-Publication Data
Phillips, Christopher, 1959 July 15–
Socrates café : A fresh taste of philosophy / by Christopher Phillips.
p. cm.
Includes bibliographical references.
ISBN 0-393-04956-6
1. Philosophy. I Title.
BD31 .P56 2001
100—dc21   00-062211

W. W. Norton & Company, Inc.
500 Fifth Avenue, New York, N.Y. 10110
www.wwnorton.com

W. W. Norton & Company Ltd.
10 Coptic Street, London WCIA 1PU

1 2 3 4 5 6 7 8 9 0

For Cecilia,
vida mia

CONTENTS

I

What Is the
Question?

Can I ask you a question?

—SOCRATES

Christopher
Phillips

"Psychiatry is the rape of the muse!"

The outburst jolts me from my reverie. I'm perched on a swivel stool in the middle of about forty-five people seated on filigreed wrought iron benches and chairs in the courtyard of an art deco café in San Francisco. It is a Tuesday night in midsummer and we're about halfway through this particular weekly gathering. We're trying to answer the question "What is insanity?"

The dialogue started out grounded in concrete examples, which quickly begged more and more questions. Was Hitler insane? Or was society itself insane at the time and did he just tap into it with cold and calculating sanity? Was Jack London insane? What about Edgar Allan Poe? And van Gogh? Was insanity a key to their genius? Is anyone who sacrifices his health for his art insane? Or is such squandering the essence of sanity? Is it sane to risk your life for something that you believe in? Or for something you don't believe in? Is a businessman sane who works all day at a job he hates? Is a society wacky that tries to prolong perpetually the lives of the terminally ill? Is a society that does not sparingly use its natural resources off its rocker? Is it nutty to have thousands of nuclear weapons poised to be launched—an act that would obliterate the planet? How can anyone be sane in this world? Or is the universe itself insane? How is the concept of insanity related to such concepts as irrationality, eccentricity, lunacy, and craziness? Is it possible to be sane and insane at the same time? Is it impossible *not* to be? Is it possible to be *completely* sane, or *completely* insane? What are the criteria for determining that someone or something is insane? Is there really any such thing as insanity?

Questions, questions, questions. They disturb. They provoke.

They exhilarate. They intimidate. They make you feel a little bit like you've at least temporarily lost your marbles. So much so that at times I'm positive that the ground is shaking and shifting under our feet. But not from an earthquake.

Welcome to Socrates Café.

Even though it is the dead of summer, it is a chilly evening. No matter. The courtyard is filled. The motley group of philosophical inquirers—aging beatniks, businesspeople, students, shopworkers, professors, teachers, palm readers, bureaucrats, and homeless persons, among others—are huddled in the middle of an ivy-laced garden. In a way, the gathering slightly resembles a church service—for heretics. And what connects us is a love for the question, and a passion for challenging even our most cherished assumptions.

All attention now is fastened on the tall, rail-thin man who lashed out against psychiatrists. He did so only after a psychiatrist said with an air of authority that the only antidote to insanity is psychiatric treatment. While the psychiatrist in question seems ruffled by the disparaging remark about his profession, his critic is sitting stock-still, the picture of calm. He has deep-set blue eyes that seem to be looking inward and a gaunt face that reveals the faintest hint of a smile. His bright red hair is neatly combed straight back except for one rebellious lock dangling over his forehead. At the moment, the only sound to be heard as we look his way is the trickling water in the gargoyle fountain.

"What do you mean?" I ask the man. "How is psychiatry the rape of the muse?"

I have an inkling that he hoped his statement would have shock value and that we would let it pass, unchallenged. Not at Socrates Café. Here we subscribe to the ethos that it is not enough to have the courage of your convictions, but you must also have the courage to have your convictions *challenged.*

It takes him some time to fix his gaze on me. "Plato spoke of a type of divine madness which he defined as 'possession by the Muses,'" he says at last, choosing his words carefully. "Plato said having this madness was indispensable to the production of the best poetry. But psychiatrists want to modify our behavior, they want us to be moderate people. They want to destroy our muse."

Christopher Phillips

"I'm a psychiatric social worker," a man quickly interjects. I expect him also to take offense at this critique of psychiatrists. But instead, with a pensive half-smile, he says, "I worry a lot about the long-range effects on people of antipsychotic medications. Just as psychiatrists try to 'cure' children with attention deficit disorder by giving them Ritalin, I think that drugs like Haldol and Zymexa and the old Thorazine are dispensed with alarming frequency to adults because of society's desire to control behavior. Moderate behavior is the god of our mental health system. To me this is chilling."

"Isn't it better to be insane than to let them kill the artist in you?" the gaunt-faced man asks his unexpected ally.

"But is it a choice between moderation and sanity?" I ask. "Can't we be a little insane, or somewhat insane, without being completely insane? In Plato's dialogue *Phaedo,* Socrates says that a *combination* of sobriety and madness impels the soul to philosophize, and I'm wondering if the same is true with art. Can't we temper the insanity within in a way that enables us to be even more in touch with our muse, and so be even more creative than we'd otherwise be able to be?"

But then I start to wonder if I know what I'm talking about. I seem to be the last person to know sane from insane. For a good while, I've been on the rather zany quest of bringing philosophy out of the universities and back "to the people," wherever they happen to be. Almost always, I do it for free. Apparently what I am doing is seen as too new, too different, too outside the norm, too . . . *crazy*. So, either for free or for a pittance, I facilitate philosophical discussions, which I call Socrates Café. I go to cafés and coffeehouses and diners. I go to day care centers, nursery schools, elementary schools, junior high and high schools, schools for special-needs children. I go to senior centers, nursing homes, assisted-living residences. I've been to a church, a hospice, a prison. I travel across the country—from Memphis to Manhattan, from Washington State to Washington, D.C.—to engage in philosophical dialogue and help others start Socrates Cafés. I pay all expenses out of my own pocket, earning a dollar here and there by other means. I often ask myself, "Am I crazy to do this?" But that is beside the point. I do not want to profit from this. This is not about money. It is a calling.

For one thing, I don't facilitate Socrates Café to teach others. I facilitate Socrates Café so others can teach *me*. The fact is that I always learn *much* more from the other participants than they could ever learn from me. Each gathering enables me to benefit from the perspectives of so many others. For another thing, you might even go so far as to say that this crazy quest of mine has *saved* my sanity. But that might be going too far. So I'll just say this: I'm seeking Socrates.

Eventually, more hands go up around the circle. The discussion heats up, gathers a certain momentum. Then a bald, stocky man with a fedora clinched in one hand jumps to his feet. "I can speak as an expert on this subject," he says. His remarkable bright green eyes seem to dance from one person to another. "I've been committed to psychiatric institutions three times since the beginning of the year. Who are they to commit me? Who are they to classify me as insane? I'm one of the sanest, smartest people I know." He remains standing.

He seems surprised that his comment is not met with shock or derision. Instead, he is peppered with questions. People want to know his story. It seems clear that most are asking themselves, "Who better to comment with insight on insanity than a person who has been labeled insane?" I am hard pressed to think of any other setting in which a group of people, most of them total strangers, would crave hearing more from someone who's just said he's certifiably insane (even if, as he insists, he's been misdiagnosed).

Then he goes on to say one of the most memorable and reasonable things I've ever heard: "Don Quixote was mad. But his madness was of a type that made him immortal. The Spanish philosopher Miguel de Unamuno said Don Quixote's legacy was . . . himself. And he wrote that 'a man, a living, eternal man, is worth all the theories and philosophies,' because in a sense he remains on earth 'and lives among us, inspiring us with his spirit.' I think that what Unamuno says of Don Quixote is even more true of Socrates. Unlike Don Quixote, Socrates apparently lived among us at one time. And he was the epitome of a rational person."

He pauses for a moment, his head now bowed. Then he looks up at all of us and says, "Socrates left us himself. He left us his wisdom and his virtue. And he remains among us, inspiring us with his spirit." We look at him in wonder.

A statuesque woman with short purple hair who is wearing a purple Green Peace T-shirt eventually asks, "Was Socrates really all that sane?"

"What do you think?" I ask her.

"Well," she replies, "when Socrates was tried and convicted of heresy for impiety and for corrupting the youth of Athens, his prosecutors hinted that if he'd agree to keep his mouth shut they wouldn't put him to death. But Socrates said he'd rather die than quit asking questions."

"Was it crazy of him to prefer death?" I ask.

"Socrates said that the unexamined life isn't worth living," she says. "So I guess for him it wasn't crazy."

"I think he *was* crazy," says a somewhat disheveled man in sandals, a Hawaiian shirt, and a battered bowler hat that completes a picture of sartorial strangeness. "But his brand of craziness has been the guide for civilizations whenever they try to set themselves on a road of sanity. Socrates was the quintessential social being. Wherever he went and engaged in dialogue, he tried to help people be more thoughtful and tolerant and rational. He wasn't insane, because his decisions were conscious and rational choices within his control. Even his decision to end his life was such a choice. But by normal societal standards he was crazy—a *good* crazy."

I end this evening's discussion on insanity by saying what I typically say at the end of every Socrates Café: "It's something to keep thinking about."

And then . . . the participants clap. Are they nuts? The discussion was intense, passionate, frustrating. Emotions were highly charged. It ended with many more questions than answers. Nothing was resolved. So why clap? I don't know, but I wind up clapping too.

SEEKING SOCRATES

Seeking Socrates? What in the world do I mean by that?

Here's the short answer: For a long time, I'd had a notion that the demise of a certain type of philosophy has been to the detriment of our society. It is a type of philosophy that Socrates and other philosophers practiced in Athens in the sixth and fifth centuries B.C. A type that utilized a method of philosophical inquiry that "everyman" and "everywoman" could embrace and take for his or her own, and in the process rekindle the childlike—but by no means childish—sense of wonder. A type of vibrant and relevant philosophy that quite often left curious souls with more questions than they'd had at the outset of the discussion, but at times enabled them to come up with at least tentative answers. A type of anti-guru philosophy in which the person leading the discussion always learns much more from the other participants than they could ever learn from him. A type of philosophy that recognized that questions often reveal more about us and the world around us than answers. A type of philosophy in which questions often *are* the answers.

But centuries ago something happened to this type of philosophy: It disappeared, for all intents and purposes. To be sure, in the eighteenth century, Voltaire held court in the gilded and red velvet setting of his favorite Parisian café—Le Procope, where he fine-tuned his ideas about reason and the development of a natural science about man. And two centuries later, in the wake of the Nazi occupation of France, Sartre developed his philosophy of existentialism under the cut-glass art deco lamps at the Café de Flore. But these cafés were reserved for the intellectual elite, who often seemed to think they had a corner on the answers. It seems safe to say that, unlike this cabal of chatterers, Socrates didn't think he knew the answers, or that knowledge was the rarified domain of so-called intellectuals. The one thing Socrates knew beyond a shadow of a doubt, he was fond of saying, was that he didn't know anything beyond a shadow of a doubt. Yet Socrates, contrary to what many think, did not try to pose as the ultimate skeptic. He wasn't trying to say that all knowledge was groundless, that we were doomed to know nothing. Rather, he was emphasizing that what he had come to know, the truths he had discovered by hard-won experience, were slippery, elusive, always tentative at best, always subject to new developments, new information, new alternatives. Every last bit of knowledge, every assumption, Socrates felt, should always be questioned, analyzed, challenged. Nothing was ever resolved once and for all.

It is with this ethos in mind that I launched Socrates Café. And the one and only firm and lasting truth that has emerged from all the Socrates Café discussions I've taken part in is that it is not possible to examine, scrutinize, plumb, and mine a question too thoroughly and exhaustively. There is always more to discover. That is the essence, and magic, of what I have come to call "Socratizing."

Socrates Café does not have to be held in a café. It can take place anywhere a group of people—or a group of one—chooses to gather and inquire philosophically. It can take place around a dining room table, in a church or a community center, on a mountaintop, in a nursing home, a hospice, a senior center, a school, a prison.

Anywhere.

Anywhere and anytime you desire to do more than regurgitate ad nauseum what you've read, or think you've read, about philosophers of the past who are considered by academics to be the undisputed exclusive members of the philosophical pantheon. It can take place anywhere people want to *do* philosophy, to *inquire philosophically*, themselves, whether with a group of people or alone.

To be sure, one of the most fruitful and flourishing places for Socrates Café to be held is at a café or coffeehouse. The gatherings typically start out small, but word spreads, and eventually more and more people come. People tell me quite frequently that "there's a hunger" for this type of discussion, that people are "weary" of the "guru approach" to group discussion. I'm not so sure about this. It seems to me that the gurus are flourishing. In fact, at one coffeehouse where I facilitated Socrates Café, while our discussion was taking place out back in the garden, tarot card readers were operating a brisk trade inside the café. Some of these mystic soothsayers seem to have been none too amused by the fact that a number of their clients, who sat with us in the garden while waiting their turn at the tarot-reading table, wound up so immersed in our dialogue that they ended up passing on the opportunity to shell out money to have their future foreseen.

Christopher Phillips

But over the short haul at least, tarot card readers and their ilk need not fear what I'm doing. For every client they lose, there are many more to take their place. There has been an upsurge of interest in the irrational the likes of which has not been seen since a similar fascination contributed to the demise of the short-lived "golden age of reason" of the ancient Greek and Roman civilizations. Millions of people still embrace such irrational phenomena as astrology. Even military commanders and politicians—even first ladies of the United States—quite often resort to this "method" to predict whether a crucial battle or competition or significant event of some other sort will have a favorable outcome. I'd argue that this modern-day embrace of the irrational reveals that overall our civilization is hardly more rational than in the days when Roman commanders sought to predict their immediate future by examining the intestines of chickens. In a way, it is startling to me that otherwise rational people can give in so easily to the temptation to see a connection between independent phenomena that happen to coincide in time. But then I recall that even the fourth-century Greek philosopher Aristotle, one of the greatest philosophers of all time, who lived amid a resurgence of belief in supernatural phenomena, was not surprised by the citizenry's pervasive love affair with the irrational. Based on his careful observations of human nature, Aristotle came to the conclusion that few men "can sustain the life of pure reason for more than very brief periods."

The classical Greek scholar E. R. Dodds noted in *The Greeks and the Irrational* that in the days of Aristotle, astrology and other irrational practices "fell upon the Hellenistic mind as a new disease falls upon some remote island." Why? "For a century or more the individual had been face to face with his own intellectual freedom. And now he turned tail and bolted from the horrid prospect—better the rigid determinism of astrological Fate than that terrifying burden of daily responsibility." The fear of and flight from freedom—which goes hand in glove with a fear of honest questioning—that is taking place today does not simply parallel what happened in ancient times. Rather, it seems to be the *same* fear and *same* flight. Today we're not so much experiencing a return of the irrational as we are an upsurgence of the irrational elements in us—such as tendencies to build belief systems on foundations of quicksand, and proclivities for destruction and self-idealization—that are part of the human fabric.

There are antidotes to the irrational. Though by no means perfect, and certainly not always skillfully handled, such antidotes can enable us to better understand ourselves, better overcome our fears, better come to grips with the irrational in us. One such antidote is the Socratic way of questioning utilized at Socrates Café. More and more people are discovering its inherent joys. They are discovering that the Socratic method can be of immense help in putting perplexities into better focus, in envisaging new directions of self-realization and human aspiration, and in pressing home the debate with the irrational.

The Socratic method of questioning aims to help people gain a better understanding of themselves and their nature and their potential for excellence. At times, it can help people make more well-informed life choices, because they now are in a better position to know themselves, to comprehend who they are and what they want. It can also enable a thoughtful person to articulate and then apply his or her unique philosophy of life. This in turn will better equip a questioning soul to engage in the endless and noble pursuit of wisdom.

Christopher
Phillips

No matter what question we discuss at Socrates Café, the dialogues, as Socrates says in Plato's *Republic,* are "not about any chance question, but about the way one should live." So the discussions do not just enable us to better know who we are but lead us to acquire new tactics for living and thinking so we can work toward determining, and then becoming, who we want to be. By becoming more skilled in the art of questioning, you will discover new ways to ask the questions that have vexed and perplexed you the most. In turn you will discover new and more fruitful answers. And these new answers in turn will generate a whole new host of questions. And the cycle keeps repeating itself—not in a vicious circle, but in an ever-ascending and ever-expanding spiral that gives you a continually new and replenished outlook on life.

Wherever Socrates Café is held, those who take part form a community of philosophical inquiry. My fellow Socratics have an enduring curiosity that cannot be quenched or satisfied by the facile responses of know-it-all gurus or of psychologists who cubbyhole their existential angst into demeaning paradigms of psychological behavior. Those who take part in Socrates Café are more concerned with formulating fruitful and reflective questions than with formulating absolute answers. Everyone is welcome and virtually all topics are valid for debate. Together, and alone, we push our thinking in surprising directions.

The possibilities are limited only by the questions your imagination and sense of wonder enable you to come up with. They don't have to be the "big questions." Or, at least, the big question may turn out to be something like "What are the big questions, and what makes them so?" During the hundreds of Socrates Cafés I've facilitated, I've often come to find that it's the unexpected, the seemingly trivial or inconsequential, or the offbeat question that might well be the most worth delving into and examining for all it's worth.

By becoming a more adept questioner, by developing a life-long love affair with the art of questioning, I'll wager that you'll be able to answer more expertly than ever that question of questions, "Who am I?"

Walt Whitman, in his poem "By Blue Ontario's Shore," wrote:

I am he who walks the States with a barb'd tongue,
questioning every one I meet.

You may not want to emulate Whitman and question every-one you meet "with a barb'd tongue," but by becoming a better questioner, by rekindling your love of questioning, you likely will develop a better sense of who you are, who you can be, where you are, why you are, and how you might want to chart a new course for yourself. You may not discover the answer that perhaps you'd anticipated, but that's part of the thrill of the search—the discovery of the unanticipated, the surprise of the novel.

The new course may be no more, and no less, than beginning the journey of philosophical inquiry. Almost without fail, new-comers to Socrates Café say enthusiastically after taking part in their first discussion, "I've been looking for something like this for so long." They discover rather quickly that engaging in what I call the Socratic quest for honesty gives their life added depth and meaning and dimensions. Asking more and better questions will give you greater personal autonomy. You will never see the world, and your place in the world, in quite the same way again as you expand your intellectual and imaginative horizons.

Contrary to popular belief, the *more* questions you have, the *firmer* the footing you are on. The *more* you know yourself. The *more* you can map out and set a meaningful path for your future.

This book is about my experiences seeking Socrates with people of all ages and all walks of life—and with myself. It is about rediscovering and tapping into my love of questions, questions, and more questions. It is about following the charge of the Delphic oracle: "Know thyself." It is not a traditional self-help book, though it might prove helpful in any number of ways. I do not pretend to be a teacher, much less a guru. Or rather, if I am a teacher, then everyone else who seeks Socrates with me is a teacher too.

The many dialogues interspersed throughout this book are real enough, though they are not rendered verbatim. I never brought along a tape recorder to any of the philosophical confabs in which I took part. What's more, the dialogues included here have had ample time to age and filter through my mind before I put pen to paper. Plato must also have added the perspectives of time and imagination when he eventually set down the "original" Socratic dialogues for posterity. In fact, he seemed to use considerable literary and philosophic license at just about every turn, in order to present even more perspectives, to make his dialogues all the more real and timeless, and to make Socrates into a figure of, some would say, mythic proportions.

As with Plato's dialogues, there's no getting around the fact that the dialogues in this book are more, and less, and other, than the "real live dialogues" they strive to depict. Most important, the ensuing dialogues are a seamless part of one great ongoing dialogue without beginning or end.

WE'RE SOCRATES

Sara Rollins arrives at the philosophical discussion group I hold each week with fourth graders at an elementary school in San Bruno, California. She is waving a somewhat crinkled piece of paper on which she'd written in pencil a single-spaced essay.

The week before, at our first gathering, the exuberant sixth grader asked me, "Who is Socrates?"

"Why don't you tell me who Socrates is when we meet again next week," I told her.

So now, the following week, after we are all seated in red plastic chairs arranged in a circle in the school library, I ask Sara, "So, who is Socrates?"

She reads from her paper: "Socrates was a Greek thinker and teacher. He was born in Athens about 469 B.C. and was put to his death there in 399. The only time he left Athens was to serve as a soldier in the Peloponnesian War. He was married to Xanthippe and had two sons. For some time Socrates worked as a sculptor and stonemason. Then he grew interested in philosophy. He spent the rest of his life thinking about philosophy and discussing it with practically everyone he met. Socrates did not teach in the regular way. He held no classes and gave no lectures and wrote no books. He simply asked questions. When he got his answer he asked more. Socrates asked his questions in order to make people think about ideas they took for granted. Some men admired this very much. They became fast friends of Socrates and joined in his philosophical discussions for many years. Others thought he was simply trying to destroy old ideas about religion and morality without putting anything in their place. Some of the young men whom he knew well became traitors to their country and led a revolution that overthrew the democratic government. The Athenians rose against them and killed them. After democracy had been restored, Socrates was brought to trial. He was accused of introducing new gods to Athens and of corrupting young men's minds. Socrates did not take these charges seriously and would not ask for mercy. So he was condemned to drinking a cup of hemlock. Many people, then and later, thought the sentence was unjust because it denied freedom of speech. Others believed that he deserved to die because his pupils nearly destroyed the Athenian state. In any case, his courage and independence have always been admired. His most famous pupil, Plato, became a great philosopher and made Socrates the chief character in most of his books."

"Wonderful," I say. We all clap.

Then Peter raises his hand. "I think Socrates is anyone who's not afraid to keep asking questions even when everyone else wants to stop him," he says.

"He's right," Sara says. And then the budding philosophical inquirer says, "We're Socrates."

WHO IS SOCRATES?

Sara is right, it seems to me.

In *The Passion of the Western Mind,* Richard Tarnas, a philosophy professor at the California Institute for Integral Studies, writes that Socrates was "imbued with a passion for intellectual honesty and moral integrity rare for his or any other age. He insistently sought answers to questions that had not before been asked, attempted to undermine conventional assumptions and beliefs to provoke more careful thinking about ethical matters, and tirelessly compelled both himself and those with whom he conversed to seek a deeper understanding of what constitutes the good life." Unlike Tarnas, I don't think Socrates asked questions that had never been asked. Rather, he devoted his life to answering certain questions in a way that had rarely before been attempted. And all those, like Sara, who in their own way try to follow in the footsteps of Socrates in both word and deed are, in a telling sense, Socrates.

And yet you still may feel inspired to ask, "Socrates who?" Because there is no definitive, unshakable proof that Socrates existed. Socrates himself never wrote down a word for posterity, as far as we know, just as Jesus never did. To be sure, you may take Plato's dialogues as hard evidence that this so-called real Socrates was faithfully depicted. There is also Xenophon's account of Socrates, as well as a comedy by Aristophanes, and there are references to Socrates in the works of Aristotle.

But the paradigmatic image is Plato's portrait. However, even in Plato's work there's no rock-solid evidence that the settings and characters Plato incorporated in the dialogues with Socrates, much less the dialogues themselves, took place in real life as Plato set them forth. Plato was a dramatist and poet and storyteller and philosopher of the life of reason. Most likely, Plato took considerable liberties.

Perhaps we can at least agree that Socrates is real to us through Plato's work, and that Plato's dialogues were truly Socratic in style and substance. And perhaps we can agree that the Socrates of Plato's dialogues stood for something special—he stood for a type of human being who engaged in unfettered, unflinching, probingly honest philosophical inquiry, a type of person who would rather be put to death than have his questioning nature muzzled.

Though I do believe he existed, and though I do believe that Plato's earliest dialogues featuring Socrates more or less accurately represent the "historical Socrates," it isn't critical to me whether he really existed, much less whether he existed precisely as Plato depicts him in the early dialogues. He surely exists as an idealized persona that we forever strive to realize within ourselves. The Socrates of whom I speak is intellectual integrity personified.

If you think this notion conflicts with some of the versions of Socrates that Plato portrayed, I do too. In some of Plato's dialogues, the Socrates that Plato limns seems to lead the other participants to an answer he already has in mind. And in some instances, he seems intentionally to try to make those who claim to know "the way, the truth, and the light" look bad or at least silly.

Just as the method that I call Socratic is ever evolving, so it is that the Socrates I'm seeking is a Socrates still to be sought and discovered in the future, not a personality primarily to be unearthed and dusted off from the past.

WHAT IS THE SOCRATIC METHOD?

The Socratic method is a way to seek truths by your own lights.

It is a system, a spirit, a method, a type of philosophical inquiry, an intellectual technique, all rolled into one.

Socrates himself never spelled out a "method." However, the Socratic method is named after him because Socrates, more than any other before or since, models for us *philosophy practiced*— philosophy as deed, as way of living, as something that any of us can do. It is an *open system* of philosophical inquiry that allows one to interrogate from many vantage points.

Gregory Vlastos, a Socrates scholar and professor of philosophy at Princeton, described Socrates' method of inquiry as "among the greatest achievements of humanity." Why? Because, he says, it makes philosophical inquiry "a common human enterprise, open to every man." Instead of requiring allegiance to a specific philosophical viewpoint or analytic technique or specialized vocabulary, the Socratic method "calls for common sense and common speech." And this, he says, "is as it should be, for how man should live is every man's business."

I think, however, that the Socratic method goes beyond Vlastos' description. It does not merely call for common sense but examines what common sense *is*. The Socratic method asks: Does the common sense of our day offer us the greatest potential for self-understanding and human excellence? Or is the prevailing common sense in fact a roadblock to realizing this potential?

Vlastos goes on to say that Socratic inquiry is by no means simple, and "calls not only for the highest degree of mental alertness of which anyone is capable" but also for "moral qualities of a high order: sincerity, humility, courage." Such qualities "protect against the possibility" that Socratic dialogue, no matter how rigorous, "would merely grind out . . . wild conclusions with irresponsible premises." I agree, though I would replace the quality of sincerity with honesty, since one can hold a conviction sincerely without examining it, while honesty would require that one subject one's convictions to frequent scrutiny.

A Socratic dialogue reveals how different our outlooks can be on concepts we use every day. It reveals how different our philosophies are, and often how tenable—or untenable, as the case may be—a range of philosophies can be. Moreover, even the most universally recognized and used concept, when subjected to Socratic scrutiny, might reveal not only that there is *not* universal agreement, after all, on the meaning of any given concept, but that every single person has a somewhat different take on each and every concept under the sun.

What's more, there seems to be no such thing as a concept so abstract, or a question so off base, that it can't be fruitfully explored at Socrates Café. In the course of Socratizing, it often turns out to be the case that some of the most so-called abstract concepts are intimately related to the most profoundly relevant human experiences. In fact, it's been my experience that virtually any question can be plumbed Socratically. Sometimes you don't know what question will have the most lasting and significant impact until you take a risk and delve into it for a while.

Christopher
Phillips

What distinguishes the Socratic method from mere nonsystematic inquiry is the sustained attempt to explore the ramifications of certain opinions and then offer compelling objections and alternatives. This scrupulous and exhaustive form of inquiry in many ways resembles the scientific method. But unlike Socratic inquiry, scientific inquiry would often lead us to believe that whatever is not measurable cannot be investigated. This "belief" fails to address such paramount human concerns as sorrow and joy and suffering and love.

Instead of focusing on the outer cosmos, Socrates focused primarily on human beings and their cosmos within, utilizing his method to open up new realms of self-knowledge while at the same time exposing a great deal of error, superstition, and dogmatic nonsense. The Spanish-born American philosopher and poet George Santayana said that Socrates knew that "the foreground of human life is necessarily moral and practical" and that "it is so even so for artists"—and even for scientists, try as some might to divorce their work from these dimensions of human existence.

Scholars call Socrates' method the *elenchus*, which is Hellenistic Greek for *inquiry* or *cross-examination*. But it is not just any type of inquiry or examination. It is a type that reveals people to themselves, that makes them see what their opinions really amount to.

C. D. C. Reeve, professor of philosophy at Reed College, gives the standard explanation of an elenchus in saying that its aim "is not simply to reach adequate definitions" of such things as virtues; rather, it also has a "moral reformatory purpose, for Socrates believes that regular elenctic philosophizing makes people happier and more virtuous than anything else. . . . Indeed philosophizing is so important for human welfare, on his view, that he is willing to accept execution rather than give it up."

Socrates' method of examination can indeed be a vital part of existence, but I would not go so far as to say that it *should* be. And I do not think that Socrates felt that habitual use of this method "makes people happier." The fulfillment that comes from Socratizing comes only at a price—it could well make us *unhappier*, more uncertain, more troubled, as well as more fulfilled. It can leave us with a sense that we *don't* know the answers after all, that we are much further from knowing the answers than we'd ever realized before engaging in Socratic discourse. And this is fulfilling—and exhilarating and humbling and perplexing. We may leave a Socrates Café—in all likelihood we *will* leave a Socrates Café—with a heady sense that there are many more ways and truths and lights by which to examine any given concept than we had ever before imagined.

In *The Gay Science*, Friedrich Nietzsche said, "I admire the courage and wisdom of Socrates in all he did, said—and did not say." Nietzsche was a distinguished nineteenth-century classical philologist before he abandoned the academic fold and became known for championing a type of heroic individual who would create a life-affirming "will to power" ethic. In the spirit of his writings on such individuals, whom he described as "Supermen," Nietzsche lauded Socrates as a "genius of the heart . . . whose voice knows how to descend into the depths of every soul . . . who teaches one to listen, who smoothes rough souls and lets them taste a new yearning . . . who divines the hidden and forgotten treasure, the drop of goodness . . . from whose touch everyone goes away richer, not having found grace nor amazed, not as blessed and oppressed by the good of another, but richer in himself, opened . . . less sure perhaps . . . but full of hopes that as yet have no name." I only differ with Nietzsche when he characterizes Socrates as someone who descended into the depths of others' souls. To the contrary, Socrates enabled those with whom he engaged in dialogues to descend into the depths of *their own* souls and create *their own* life-affirming ethic.

Santayana said that he would never hold views in philosophy which he did not believe in daily life, and that he would deem it dishonest and even spineless to advance or entertain views in discourse which were not those under which he habitually lived. But there is no neat divide between one's views of philosophy and of life. They are overlapping and kindred views. It is virtually impossible in many instances to *know* what we believe in daily life until we engage others in dialogue. Likewise, to discover our philosophical views, we must engage with ourselves, with the lives we already lead. Our views form, change, evolve, as we participate in this dialogue. It is the only way truly to discover what philosophical colors we sail under. Everyone at some point preaches to himself and others what he does not yet practice; everyone acts in or on the world in ways that are in some way contradictory or inconsistent with the views he or she confesses or professes to hold. For instance, the Danish philosopher Søren Kierkegaard, the influential founder of existentialism, put Socratic principles to use in writing his dissertation on the concept of irony in Socrates, often using pseudonyms so he could argue his own positions with himself. In addition, the sixteenth-century essayist Michel de Montaigne, who was called "the French Socrates" and was known as the father of skepticism in modern Europe, would write and add conflicting and even contradictory passages in the same work. And like Socrates, he believed the search for truth was worth dying for.

The Socratic method forces people "to confront their own dogmatism," according to Leonard Nelson, a German philosopher who wrote on such subjects as ethics and theory of knowledge until he was forced by the rise of Nazism to quit. By doing so, participants in Socratic dialogue are, in effect, "*forcing* themselves to be free," Nelson maintains. But they're not just confronted with their own dogmatism. In the course of a Socrates Café, they may be confronted with an array of hypotheses, convictions, conjectures and theories offered by the other participants, and themselves—all of which subscribe to some sort of dogma. The Socratic method requires that—honestly and openly, rationally and imaginatively—they confront the dogma by asking such questions as: What does this mean? What speaks for and against it? Are there alternative ways of considering it that are even more plausible and tenable?

At certain junctures of a Socratic dialogue, the "forcing" that this confrontation entails—the insistence that each participant carefully articulate her singular philosophical perspective—can be upsetting. But that is all to the good. If it never touches any nerves, if it doesn't upset, if it doesn't mentally and spiritually challenge and perplex, in a wonderful and exhilarating way, it is not Socratic dialogue. This "forcing" opens us up to the varieties of experiences of others—whether through direct dialogue, or through other means, like drama or books, or through a work of art or a dance. It compels us to explore alternative perspectives, asking what might be said for or against each.

Keep this ethos in mind if you ever, for instance, feel tempted to ask a question like this one once posed at a Socrates

Café: How can we overcome alienation? Challenge the premise of the question at the outset. You may need to ask: Is alienation something we always *want* to overcome? For instance, Shakespeare and Goethe may have written their timeless works because they embraced their sense of alienation rather than attempting to escape it. If this was so, then you might want to ask: Are there many different types, and degrees, of alienation? Depending on the context, are there some types that you want to overcome and other types that you do not at all want to overcome but rather want to incorporate into yourself? And to answer effectively such questions, you first need to ask and answer such questions as: What is alienation? What does it *mean* to overcome alienation? Why would we ever want to overcome alienation? What are some of the many different types of alienation? What are the criteria or traits that link each of these types? Is it possible to be completely alienated? And many more questions besides.

Those who become smitten with the Socratic method of philosophical inquiry thrive on the question. They never run out of questions, or out of new ways to question. Some of Socrates Café's most avid philosophizers are, for me, the question personified.

A DIALOGUE OF ONE

It is nearly midnight and I am making my way home after facilitating a Socrates Café at Mad Magda's Russian Tea Room in the heart of San Francisco. It is only the second time I've facilitated Socrates Café at this eclectic establishment, yet more than fifty people have come each time. And each time I notice that a good many of the people who attend the discussion come alone, and seem to know few if any of the others who are on hand to take part. Yet after the discussion has formally ended, many cluster in small groups, talking with one another as if they are fast friends. The previous week, after discussing the question "What is enough?" I joined one of the clusters. But this week I join the ten or so folks who choose to beat a rather hasty retreat after the intense discussion comes to an end. I am anxious to be alone with my thoughts, to tend to the many questions in my mind that were generated by the dialogue.

The question into which we delved this evening was "Why question?" This question was posed only after a number of other intriguing ones were pitched, including: "Is there such a thing as human nature?" "What if anything is the nature of individuality?" "When is life not worth living?" "What is the nature of transcendence?" "Does human nature vary across time or cultures?" But then a striking teenage girl with hair that fell to her ankles said, "Why question?" Until then she'd seemed more intent on gabbing with her friends than listening to the questions being proposed. We turned to her almost in unison. She looked at us all with a Mona Lisa–like smile, as if she had only been biding her time and somehow knew we'd pick her question— which we did.

Why question? Perhaps we don't have a choice, according to John Dewey, a leading American philosopher, educator, and social reformer, who noted that Socrates said we are "questioning beings" who "must search out the reason of things, and not accept them from custom and authority." As Gerasimos Xenophon Santas, who was chairman of the philosophy department at the University of California–Irvine, noted in his study of Plato's early

Socratic dialogues, "Socrates is questioning all the time. He greets people with questions, he teaches and refutes them with questions, he leaves them with questions—he actually talks to them with questions." Even when he isn't talking, Socrates seems to be "holding a silent question-and-answer session" with an imaginary interlocutor. It really seems as if Socrates, for one, has no choice but to question. But most people, at least adults, seem to have to make that choice.

The question "Why question?" turned out to be a much harder question to answer than perhaps any of us at this Socrates Café had presumed. The problem was, in order to answer it, we first needed to see if we were on the same page in terms of what a question means, is, does, and can do.

It seemed most of us taking part in this dialogue had taken for granted that we all thoroughly understood the concept of question. But judging from the wildly diverse responses that followed, each of us had a very different take on what precisely a question is and what purpose it serves.

"People only ask questions if they already know what answer they want" was the firm conviction of a woman who was sitting apart from the rest of the group. Her bright blond hair was in curlers and mostly covered by a lavender scarf that seemed to be patterned with amoebas. "For instance," she went on, "if a woman asks you, 'How's my hair?' she doesn't want you to tell her the truth if it looks bad. She wants you to say, 'It looks wonderful.'"

Needless to say, many others disagreed and said that just the opposite was true, that people only ask questions if they don't know the answer. "People ask questions out of curiosity, out of wonder," said a burly man with a raspy voice and extraordinarily arched brows. He had been stirring his coffee since long before the discussion began, and he had yet to take a sip. "I don't know of anyone who would ask a question if they already knew what they wanted the answer to be."

The woman wouldn't hear of it. "People know that curiosity and wonder always get you in trouble," she said, for some reason snapping her fingers in the process. "So if they don't already know, or feel pretty sure they know, what the answer is, they don't ask the question."

"I think that may be true in some cases," said the willowy teenage girl whose question we were discussing. Again, she hadn't seemed to be paying attention at all, so absorbed was she in a conversation with her friends; but she had been listening to every word. "But in *all* cases?" she went on. "How would we ever have new and unexpected discoveries if we only asked questions to which we already knew the answer?"

"That's a loaded question," the woman with curlers replied. "If I disagree with you," she then said, her glance volleying between the teenage girl and the burly man, "you'll think I'm just being stubborn. And if I agree with what you just said, you'll think I've seen the error of my ways and that you've won me over. It's like asking a man, 'Did you stop beating your wife?' There's no fair way to answer that. You're damned if you do and damned if you don't."

The teenage girl looked baffled. "I don't see how what you just said has anything to do with . . ." But before she could complete her sentence one of her friends interjected, "Many scientists find answers to questions that were not even asked. Such as the accidental discovery of penicillin. That was found while altogether different questions were being asked. So questions are used for experimentation and in many cases they lead to unanticipated answers."

"One of the biggest dangers lies with not asking questions," said an electrical engineer whose somber suit matched his countenance. "Because that practice limits knowledge. It leads to closed minds and closed societies."

Christopher Phillips

"What you say brings to mind that character Yossarian in Joseph Heller's *Catch-22*," says another participant. "He was described as a 'collector of good questions,' which he used to 'wring knowledge' out of people. But his superiors in his American bomber squadron always tried to shut him up whenever he began to ask questions because they felt 'there was no telling what people might find out once they felt free to ask whatever questions they wanted to.' Yossarian's superiors thought questions were subversive, to be avoided at all costs. So what happened was a colonel enacted a rule that only permitted people who never asked questions to ask questions. Catch-22. I wonder sometimes if that's where we're headed."

The last remark of the evening came from a diffident and somewhat finicky young man wearing a red and white beanie and a faded T-shirt. A regular Socrates Café–goer no matter where the event is held, he always asks penetrating questions. "Doesn't it seem like if we did nothing else the entire evening but ask one question after another, we might reveal more about who we are than if we tried to answer any one of them?" he asked. His insight rang true for me, and judging by the thoughtful looks on many other faces, I suspect it rang true for most of the other participants as well.

And now that the discussion is over, I'm anxious to be alone so I can ponder the question he raised. While driving home, I ask myself, "What questions have I been asking myself of late?"

It strikes me that a question that just won't go away has been ... What is it I fear? Often it seems that fear prevents people from asking questions of themselves or others. Before I began regularly facilitating Socrates Café far and wide, I feared being alone. But now that Socratizing has caught on like I never dreamed, and consequently I am in constant demand and have been facilitating upwards of ten philosophical discussions each week at cafés and nursing homes and schools and universities, I seem to fear not having enough time alone. So I have come to cherish the time I spend alone after Socrates Café. After an intensive dialogue, there's nothing I like better than the stark counterpoint of being by myself.

But tonight, no sooner do I open the front door to my apartment than the phone rings.

"Hello?" I say, hoping it is a telemarketer so I can quickly hang up. A barely audible voice on the other end says, "I came to the Socrates Café tonight. I hope it's okay to call you."

"Sure," I say without conviction as I make a mental note to get an unlisted number.

"I didn't say a word during the discussion," she then says, her voice wavering. She doesn't tell me her name and I don't think to ask. "I just don't like to talk in groups."

"That's quite all right," I say. "As you probably noticed, I never put anyone on the spot and make them feel like they have to talk. You can participate just by listening. In fact, I find that some of the most active participants at Socrates Café are often those who 'just' listen."

There is a long pause—so long that I think she might be through talking. In fact, I hope I've said whatever needed to be said to bring this conversation to a quick end. But then she says, "I'm calling because I want to know if you think it's possible for me to have a Socrates Café by myself."

A solo Socrates Café? A *tête-à-tête* with only one *tête*?

"Yes," I tell her. "Absolutely."

"How?" she asks immediately.

"I bet you already hold a Socrates Café of sorts with yourself from time to time," I say.

"?" she replies wordlessly.

"I don't really think there's much difference in having a dialogue in public, like Socrates Café, and the inner dialogue that we have with ourselves much of the time," I say. "Hannah Arendt once wrote that Socrates 'makes public in discourse the thinking process—the dialogue that soundlessly goes on within me, between me and myself.' And I think this is very much the case.

"I bet you ask yourself questions all the time," I go on to say, "and that you make heartfelt attempts not only to answer these questions but to examine the answers you come up with from many different angles and perspectives. For instance, I bet you don't realize how often you question who you are, who you want to be, and try to come up with a number of 'answers.'"

"Well . . ." she says, "I suppose that's true enough." She goes silent on the other end of the line. But eventually my phone correspondent says, "Lately I can't sleep at nights because I keep asking myself, 'What is the meaning of life?'" There's another pause before she says, "Actually, I don't so much ask myself the question as the question just sort of appears. And it seems like there's nothing I can do to make it go away, even when I try to answer it."

She pauses yet again. "I guess I should back up a bit," she then says. "My niece died of leukemia several months ago. She was fourteen. She was a truly gifted child. One of those children who could've gone on to excel in practically any field. Our nearest and dearest always said how much alike she and I were. When I was a child everyone used to say the sky was the limit for me. I liked studying everything, and excelled in everything—so much so that I could never figure out one thing that I'd like to do or be. But . . .

well, I guess there's no 'but.' The long and short of it is: that became a moot point. I ended up getting married at nineteen. I dropped out of college because my husband didn't want me to work. We got divorced thirteen years later. Now I work as a bookkeeper. I feel . . . well, I don't know what I feel. I don't feel comfortable saying any more about this, except to say that the 'What is the meaning to life?' question won't go away. So I don't get much sleep these days."

The woman does not say anything more to me for a short while. I suspect that she feels, like me, that the lull in our conversation is a comfortable and even necessary one. "I don't really know, though . . ." she reflects after a while. "Like I said, I can never come up with any sort of satisfying answer to the question 'What's the meaning of life?'

"No, that's not it," she sighs. "I don't even know how to begin to answer the question."

"Maybe you're not asking the question in the right way," I say.

"What do you mean?"

"Maybe," I say, "before you try to answer the question as you've posed it—or as it's been posed to you—maybe you first need to ask and answer other questions."

"Like what?"

"Like 'Whose life am I talking about?' Are you talking about 'what is the meaning of life?' as it relates to your life? If so, you need to say so explicitly."

"I think what I'm really trying to ask is 'What gives my life meaning?'" she says.

"There you go!" I say. I am surprised by how enthused I am that she has discovered this 'new way' of asking the question, particularly since I'd been so reluctant to talk. But the one thing that has ceased to surprise me about Socratic dialogue is how it so often invigorates and even rejuvenates me. I no longer am in a hurry to hang up the phone and be alone. "This new way of asking the question may lead to a more promising answer."

Then she says, "Oh no."

"What?" I say. I worry I've somehow inadvertently offended her.

"The way I put the question didn't really explain what I mean by *meaning*. So now I think I've come up with a better way to ask it." She sounds apologetic.

"That's wonderful," I say, impressed that she has already become a more critical questioner. "Let's hear it."

"What I think I'm really trying to ask is 'What can I do to give my life the kind of meaning that makes my spirit soar, that makes me feel like I'm making this world at least a little bit better place to live in?'" The tone of her voice becomes more and more upbeat and even excited as she formulates the question—as if the question itself is an epiphany for her.

"That's a beautiful question," I tell her. "I don't know the answer, but I bet you'll figure it out, now that you've posed it this way. And I'll bet you'll come up with many more questions, and answers, as you further pursue this line of questioning."

She breathes what seems to be a sigh of relief.

I then go on to say, "It seems to me that no matter what question you ask yourself, whether completely alone or with other people, if you give it your all when you try to answer it, you are trying to better understand yourself. And self-understanding can be self-transcendence. It can put your life in new perspectives. You can see your place in the scheme of things from new vistas and vantage points, because you are further discovering your mind. And discovering your mind can be like discovering a new universe.

"What's more, new questions have the potential to lead to new discoveries," I continue. "They can have a huge impact on your life. Answering a question like the one you're posing now requires that you use your imagination. It requires that you dare to think up compelling alternatives to ways you're currently going about life and living. It requires that you take risks with your thinking. And then the even harder work would involve taking concrete steps toward making your imaginative vision a reality."

"I see what you mean," she says. "Or at least I think I do." She laughs loud and rather long, and for the first time does not seem the least bit self-conscious. She is excited. She says, "Until just now I hadn't realized that I've been so frustrated because I haven't asked the question in a way that would ever lead me to any sort of meaningful answers."

"There're no shortcuts to the questioning life," I say. "I think the questioning life in many ways is the 'examined life' Socrates talked about: It's hard work—trying to figure out new ways, better ways, to ask the questions that perplex you the most, so you can come up with more meaningful and fruitful answers.

"But you don't need a community outside yourself to do this. At times it might be helpful, though. And there are many other kinds of viable communities besides the type of community at Socrates Café. Like the 'community' of world literature. I know that by reading books such as Ford Madox Ford's *The Good Soldier* and Robert Musil's *The Man Without Qualities* and Hermann Broch's *The Guiltless*, I discovered a number of perspectives on human nature that I most likely would never have come upon any other way. And these perspectives helped me give more meaning to my own life."

"Books like Dostoevsky's *Notes from the Underground* and Ralph Ellison's *Invisible Man* and Elias Canetti's *Auto da Fé* have had the same sort of impact on me," she replies. "Reading books like that made me ask questions about my life, and about

33

humanity in general, that I'd probably never have asked without reading them."

"So you see? You're already further on your way than you realized," I tell her as I try to imagine what she looks like, the expression on her face. "Asking questions can enable you to experiment, to try on for size different ways of seeing.

"That's what I do when I catechize myself with variations of the 'What is the meaning of life?' question. I don't simply try to come up with a definitive answer right away to whatever way I've formulated this question. Instead, I try to come up with a number of different points of view, a number of potential answers. I play devil's advocate with myself. And then I ask myself, 'What speaks for, and against, each of these perspectives?'

"In fact," I continue, "only after years of asking and attempting to answer variations of the question 'How can I give my life the kind of meaning that makes my life worthwhile for me?' did I come to the realization that the only life for me was to be sort of a Johnny Appleseed of philosophers. My questions took years to bear fruit. And it took even longer, once I had some tentative answers, to transform thought into deed. But once I started the journey, I wouldn't have dreamed of quitting. And my life has gone in the most exhilarating directions."

I finally pause to draw a breath. I've said more than enough. As I wait to see if my anonymous caller has something more to say, I realize just how much this conversation has put me in a more focused frame of mind for my own self-questioning.

"You know what I'm going to do?" she says to me at long last. Without waiting for a reply, she says, "I'm going to make myself a cup of coffee, then go sit out on the back porch and spend the rest of the night thinking of new ways to ask, and answer, 'What is the meaning of life?'"

Her voice is no longer timid and wavering. I can almost hear her smile. But before I have a chance to urge her on, I hear a click, then a buzzing. She has hung up. I doubt she even realizes what she's done. After all, it's just dawned on her that she has a lot of Socratic questioning to do.

As do I.

II

Where Am I?

I sought myself.

—HERACLITUS, SIXTH-CENTURY GREEK PHILOSOPHER

THE MISEXAMINED LIFE

Christopher
Phillips

"Why did you start Socrates Café?"

The wide-eyed and winsome woman who asks me this question is clutching a cell phone in one hand. Even though it is quite warm inside, she has not removed her heavy blue wool coat, as if she might have to leave at any moment. She is among eighteen curious souls who have shown up for the first-ever Socrates Café I am inaugurating at the Borders bookstore in Wayne, New Jersey. A month earlier, I had approached the bookstore's "community relations coordinator" with my idea of bringing back to life the kinds of dialogue Socrates held with groups of people way back when. I told her I'd set my sights on the café section of the bookstore for this philosophical discussion group. To my delight, the initial response was an encouraging "Wow." Then she said, "What do you want to call it?"

What a question. It never occurred to me that it needed to be called something. I just knew I wanted to start a philosophical discussion group at a café. I just knew it was to be a café for the Socrates in us. "Let's call it Socrates Café," I said.

And now here we are, sitting around three square tables pushed together in the café section of the bookstore. I am perched in the middle on a stool.

"Well, the short answer to your question is, I started it because I agree with Socrates that 'the unexamined life is not worth living,'" I say to the woman who asked about Socrates Café's genesis.

Her look was both critical and quizzical. "What does he mean, 'the unexamined life is not worth living'?"

"What do you think he means?" I ask.

"I have no idea," she says. " I've spent years overexamining my life, going to one psychotherapist after another. I think it might've been better if I'd never started examining my life in the first place. All the years in psychotherapy have not helped me live a better life today. So if Socrates is saying that only the examined life is worth living, I don't know if he knew what he was talking about."

"I think Socrates was talking specifically about the philosophically examined life," says a dour, burly man with an ill-kempt mustache who is sitting well back from the table, as if he wants to create some distance between himself and the rest of the group. He has a nervous habit of rapidly circling his thumbs round and round one another.

"What is the philosophically examined life?" I ask.

"It's a life where you are always trying to answer the question 'Who am I?'" says a soft-spoken man with tired brown eyes and long white hair tied in a ponytail. He has just joined the gathering. He has in hand a dog-eared copy of Plato's Socratic dialogues.

One man, a recently retired army lieutenant, then says, "I think it's pointless to examine your life, philosophically or otherwise. Hindsight is always twenty-twenty. If you spend time brooding over your past, you're not living in the present. My older brother spends every second of every day regretting what he didn't do in the past. What good does it do? It doesn't change anything. It just keeps him from living now."

A slightly built man who has been smiling nervously throughout the discussion, suddenly quits smiling and shakes his head. "I disagree that it's pointless to take stock of your life," he says. "If you don't examine your life, you can never make changes that'll make life more fulfilling here and now. You need to look at the decisions you made and ask, how can I do it better next time? You don't do it to feel guilty or to be too hard on yourself, but to give today more meaning."

"Well," I say, "I for one can say that examining your life does not necessarily make for a more meaningful today. After examining my life, I decided it was not worth living."

They ask me to tell them more. I go on to tell this group of strangers that before I made the commitment to start Socrates Café both my personal and professional life had ceased to have meaning for me. Many of my nearest and dearest would have been surprised by this revelation. Many of them envied my life. For over a decade, I had been a writer for national magazines. I traveled a great deal, met fascinating people. But I was deeply unhappy. I frequently asked myself: 'Why can't I just be normal and accept the fact that jobs are not meant to be all that fulfilling? Why can't I just accept the fact that most adults end up abandoning their more youthful and idealistic aspirations?' The answer I came up with was always the same: Because life is not a dress rehearsal. Because I shouldn't settle for less than doing exactly what I want to do with my life, despite the risks, or, better, because of the risks. My philosophy of life had always been to live intensely, to love intensely. But I hadn't done that. Though the life of a freelance writer is an intense and precarious one in its way, for me it was still playing it too safe. For a long time I lived in that seductive world of "If only . . ." I was mired in regret over what I hadn't done. And I spent no time trying to change my life here and now. Nietzsche said something to the effect that one should strive to live dangerously, and I think what he meant was that we shouldn't hesitate to take sublime risks with our lives. I'd always intended to take such risks, but I hadn't.

I go on to tell the group, "At a time of despair, I asked myself: 'Where is Socrates?'"

At this, their looks range from quizzical to bemused. I smile and say, "Now, I realize this isn't what most people ask themselves in time of despair. But this is the question that came to my mind.

And what I meant was 'Where is the Socrates in me?' Or, to put it another way, 'What happened to my childlike love affair with questions?'"

Then I say, "I'd long had this notion of resuscitating the type of community Socrates had created—a community of questioners. But I had always put roadblocks in my way. I'd always come up with some sort of clever excuse not to do it. But I'd reached a point where I literally couldn't go on living a life that I felt was in too many ways a lie. I had run out of excuses."

I look at the other participants, who in turn are looking at me quite intently. I say, "And that's why we're here now."

"So shit happens, and sometimes because of the shit that happens, you kill yourself," says a teenage girl with spiked hair, orange lipstick that matches the color of her hair, and a number of pierced rings in various parts of her body. "And other times, you make big changes in your life that make it worthwhile enough to go on living."

I smile. "That sounds about right to me."

The man with Plato's dialogues in hand says, "I ask myself each day, 'Is my life worthwhile enough not to commit suicide?'" He goes on to say that he now spends summers and the Christmas holiday working for UPS, and the rest of the year he travels around the world. "It is the only life that is worth living, for me," he says.

The woman who started off our conversation says, "I'm an executive of a corporation. I make a six-figure income. I'm 'successful.' But more often than not, I'm deeply unhappy. I have to say, though, that coming here tonight and working my brain again in a way I never have a chance to do at work or at home or with a therapist makes me feel . . . better." Several others nod.

A gaunt, lanky young man inches his chair closer and closer to us as the conversation progresses. He has been sitting a table away from us, half reading a book by Dostoevsky, half listening to our conversation. Now he says, "I think Socrates wasn't really saying all that much when he said 'the unexamined life is not worth living.' I think it's impossible not to examine your life. Only someone with a lobotomy could go through life without examining it. To me the question isn't whether or not I should examine my life, but how I should examine it."

"I agree," I say. "But so far, in examining the question 'What is the examined life?' we've only talked about it in relation to examining ourselves. But that's not all there is to it, is it? I mean, if we're really talking about examining life from a number of perspectives, don't we have to examine life outside ourselves as well? How can we understand who we are if we don't try to understand the universe all around us as well as the universe inside of us?"

"Well, there's lots of fields where people try to examine life," says an earnest young woman who told me before our discussion got under way that she's been accepted in the Ph.D. program in philosophy at Harvard but isn't sure the academic way is how she wants to devote her life to doing philosophy. "Because every time there's a new discovery or a new theory or a new invention, we have a better idea who we are and what we're capable of. But I think that what separates philosophy from science is that science moves, as Roger Scruton wrote, 'from the observed to the unobserved to the unobservable. Science can't address the 'why' of its subjects. This is the domain of philosophy. And in addressing the why, we begin the search for both a reason and a meaning. There cannot be a scientific examination of personhood or the beautiful or the good life. These are uniquely the challenge of examining life philosophically. And I don't think anyone better met that challenge than Socrates."

"You know what I think?" says a woman who works at the café. She has had an unlit cigarette dangling between her lips throughout the discussion. She takes the cigarette out of her mouth, points it at me, and then says, "I think that only by examining your life in every way possible can you be said to be examining your life philosophically."

"Every way possible?" says a man with a severe manner who is wearing a bright yellow Hertz Rent A Car windbreaker and who has been pretending to thumb through a copy of *People* magazine throughout the conversation. "I don't think that's either possible or necessary. For one thing, how would you ever know if you had examined your life 'every way possible'? And even if you could, wouldn't you be overwhelmed by the attempt, and so busy examining your life 'every way possible' that you'd never get around to the business of living your life?"

This observation gives the café employee pause. But then, choosing her words carefully, she says, "Well, I think what I meant to say—and didn't say very well—was that this way of examining your life that we're using here seems to require that you leave yourself open to new ways of examining your life—and by that I mean new perspectives, new methods, things like that. I think that's the method Socrates tried to model, and that Aristotle and so many others have adopted for their own uses and interests."

"I think you're right," says the man, closing his magazine. "And maybe we shouldn't expect to do more than what we're doing right here."

HERE, HERE!

But . . . where and what is "here"?

Most of the seekers I've encountered often seem to be asking: Why am I where I am? Another way of asking this is: What is my place in the scheme of things? Yet another way is to ask: Why am I here?

René Descartes, a French mathematician who is considered the father of modern philosophy, attempted to extend mathematical method to all knowledge in his quest for certainty. It was his

Christopher Phillips

ability to think that led him to conclude that he was in fact here, hence his famous aphorism "I think, therefore I am." A significantly different view was held by the eighteenth-century German philosopher Immanuel Kant, whose influential "critical philosophy" asserted that ideas do not necessarily conform to the external world, but rather the world is known only to the extent to which it conforms with the human mind's structure. To Kant, what was imperative was to know *why* he was here. In his *Critique of Pure Reason,* Kant tried to shed light on this question by asking and attempting to answer what he felt were three critical questions: What can I know? What ought I to do? What may I hope? Friedrich Nietzsche felt that each person had to discover his singular *why*—his unique station in life—in order to make the slings and arrows of life worth bearing. "He who has a *why* to live," he wrote, "can bear with almost any *how.*"

Socrates operated on the assumption that he was a thinking being who was indeed *here*. He felt that the *why,* the singular reason for his existence, was to ask and answer questions that would enable him to become a more virtuous person.

There are many fruitful ways to frame these "foundational questions." For instance, you might feel compelled to ask ... Do I *have* to be here? Or, How can I get from here to there? Or, Are there other "heres" besides this here? Why am I *not* fully here? Is there anything I *must* do while I'm here? How can I best use the time while I'm here so that when I'm no longer here, those who come after me will know beyond a doubt "*I was here!*"? You likely can think of more and even better ways to ask, and answer, Why am I here?

To gain insight into such questions, Socrates Café–goers subject their beliefs, their worldviews, to cogent objections and alternatives. They recognize that philosophical inquiry requires each of us to evaluate radically and continually our beliefs, our lives, our selves, our place. They refuse to accept any class of so-called truths at face value. They think it's always open to debate whether a certain set of beliefs is humane or rational, wise or good. And they clearly believe that it is up to them to discover their place in the world.

Can every single soul better discover her unique person and place by taking part in Socrates Café? I don't know. Is Socratic philosophical inquiry *the* one and only legitimate form of inquiry for such self-discovery? No way. But everyone, whether he or she realizes it or not, or has articulated it or not, has a philosophy of life, and of place. Whether or not we are partially aware, or wholly aware, of our "philosophical approach to life and living," virtually everything we think, every action we take, every move we make, whether fateful or mundane, reflects in some way our worldview and our worldplace.

A GATHERING PLACE

I arrive at the church in Northern California before the Sunday service has ended. I don't mind waiting. I can hear the congregation singing soothing hymns inside the big peach-colored building, built on the model of an old Spanish monastery. It brings back pleasant childhood memories of the times I went with my mom to the Methodist church she attended. I notice that the sign outside the entrance of the stately edifice pronounces in large white letters that it is a "liberal religious community." The sign does not so much as mention that this is a church.

Christopher
Phillips

I have been invited here to facilitate a Socrates Café by a woman who has attended discussions I've held at a senior center. Fifteen minutes later, I am in the church's cozy meeting room along with about twenty members of the congregation. Most sit on comfortable sofas and chairs that line the walls. I sit on the edge of a recliner to avoid being swallowed up by its plush cushion.

"Welcome," the woman who invited me then says to me. "I was going to say, 'Welcome to our church,' but many of us don't even think of this as a church." Most of the others nod or murmur their agreement.

"If you don't mind," I say, "I'm wondering if you will help me answer the question 'What is a church?'" I rarely pick a topic myself for discussion, but am glad to find they are quite willing, even enthusiastic, to take on this question.

A woman who says she's a longtime member of the church tells me, "I honestly couldn't give you a definition of a church. I'm afraid I'm going to have to look it up." She smiles, accentuating her kind looks. Then she goes to a bookshelf and pulls out a huge careworn Webster's dictionary. She thumbs through it until she reaches the page she's looking for. She reads to herself for a moment and then says, "It says here that the one thing all churches have in common is that they're all houses of worship for Christians."

"But I'm not a Christian," says one man, an engineer, with light skin and ruddy cheeks. "I'm a spiritual agnostic—I believe there's a supreme force of some sort, but I'm not at all sure I'd call this force 'God.' And no one here is troubled or offended by my outlook. Our sect is for everyone, not just Christians." Then he looks my way and says, "No one has ever made me feel the least bit uncomfortable here. In fact, people often joke to me, 'How's our resident agnostic?' I feel like part of a family here."

A somewhat diffident man who is sitting next to me on a sofa with his wife says to me, "We're considering changing the name of our gathering place from 'church' to 'congregation.'"

"Why?" I ask.

"They feel that the word 'congregation' more faithfully represents what we're all about," he says. "Because just like the dictionary says, a church is equated with Christians. And we want everyone to feel welcome, Christian, Muslim, agnostic, what have you."

Then he says, "I think all of us are religious, but not in the way that people are who are members of the traditional Christian denominations. I think most of us believe in a supreme being or higher power of some sort who is our raison d'être and who looks over us and guides us. But our beliefs about who or what this supreme being or higher power is, and how we show our spiritual humility and reverence to him or her or it, run the gamut."

His remarks on what he deems a religious person to be seem to gibe with the outlook of the Protestant theologian Friedrich Ernst Schleiermacher, who said that the "essence" of being a religious person is "the feeling of an absolute dependence." In *The Future of an Illusion*, Sigmund Freud registered his objection to Schleiermacher's view when he wrote, "It is not this feeling [of absolute dependence] that constitutes the essence of religiousness, but only the next step, the reaction to it, which seeks a remedy against this feeling. He who goes no further, he who humbly resigns himself to the insignificant part man plays in the universe, is, on the contrary, irreligious in the truest sense of the word."

"Some may say it sounds as if you are trying to go to great lengths to distance yourself from the typical idea most people have of churches," I say.

"Absolutely," he replies.

"The thing is," says the avowed agnostic, "we're open to just about anything. And we welcome people to join the church here, to become members, even if they've made it clear that not only are they not diehard Christians, but that they may not believe in any sort of god at all. I'm a great example of that. We're open to anyone."

IT TAKES A COMMUNITY

In the days and weeks to come, I continued to think a great deal more about the Socratic dialogue at the church. It seemed that the common thread among all the folks there who engaged with me was their desire to be part of a certain type of community where they felt comfortable regardless of their disparate religious views. I began to think that their characterization of the church as a congregation was very similar to how I'd characterize Socrates Café gatherings: they too are congregations of a sort. I know that most people who attend regularly can't imagine life without the weekly gatherings, and I'm sure most of those at the church feel the same way. I myself use the same sort of language to greet people at Socrates Café that a minister might use at a church service. All of us old-timers greet each other with hugs and handshakes, and I come up to newcomers and shake their hands and say, "Thanks for coming." At the end of the discussions I make a point to find them and tell them I hope they'll come back. Many do. They find that this is precisely the type of community they've been looking to be a part of, just as those at the church congregation feel that that is a type of community that they would not want to be without.

I've often characterized Socrates Café as a "church service for heretics," a place where we all feel comfortable challenging our respective dogmas. In his essay "Creative Democracy," John Dewey writes: "I am inclined to believe that the heart and final guarantee of democracy is in free gatherings of neighbors on the street corner to discuss back and forth . . . and converse freely with one another. . . . For everything which bars freedom and fullness of communication sets up barriers that divide human beings into sets and cliques . . . and thereby undermines the democratic way of life."

But I'm not at all sure that free gatherings of freely conversing neighbors are the sole guarantors of a robust democracy. I think the *way* people go about conversing is every bit as critical as their ability to converse freely. If, for instance, they all speak freely and fully in a series of non sequiturs, if they don't react to and critically examine and build upon one another's perspectives, it seems they may be left with a rather empty and stagnant type of democracy. When Dewey calls for the "freedom and fullness of communication," he does hint that a certain type of dialogue may be necessary to preserve democracy. While he doesn't precisely say what he means, I think the Socratic way of inquiring is a paradigm of communication that calls on all participants in a dialogue to participate fully, and in an egalitarian way. And it requires that participants help one another articulate and then examine their perspectives, as well as the implications for society of these perspectives, and the assumptions within these perspectives. This, I think, is a type of "free and full" communication that can help ensure a vibrant democracy that can evolve over time.

Christopher
Phillips

I think that Dewey—who throughout his career emphasized the importance of inquiry in the pursuit of knowledge—would consider the type of inquiry that takes place at Socrates Café critical to bolstering a democratic way of life. But many find such gatherings anathema. In fact, ever since the days of ancient Athens, the brand of philosophical inquiry originated by Socrates has had more than its share of naysayers. They carp that it is not pious, positive, and jingoistic enough. They complain that the type of persistent, probing inquiry epitomized by Socrates is a roadblock to what they call the acquisition of "the Truth."

How do those of us who practice this type of philosophical inquiry plead? Guilty as charged. Socrates felt it was our duty to inquire relentlessly. For him it was a moral injunction. This "Socratic ethos" is inseparable from the Socratic method itself. In distinguishing Socrates from the Sophists of his day—the philosophers who like Socrates took to the Athenian streets to philosophize, but who unlike Socrates charged an arm and a leg for their "wisdom"—Laszlo Versenyi, professor of philosophy at Williams College, wrote:

> The Sophists gave lectures. Socrates "merely" questioned. The Sophists gave verbal exhibitions on education, virtue, and human excellence. Socrates exhibited them by embodying them in his life. . . . [He] brought about internal improvement in men, a true "therapy for the soul." . . . It was painful to undergo his questioning, to experience the pangs of intellectual growth. . . . Socrates emphasized wisdom, held lack of insight to be lack of worth. . . . He was not a detached inquirer into things alien to us but a man completely involved in his inquiry.

Those over the ensuing years who have taken the Socratic ethos for their own have tended to be the "bad conscience" of their times. From Galileo to Gandhi, Solzhenitsyn to Rosa Parks, there have always been those few who have openly and forcefully questioned and challenged the conventional "wisdom" of their era. There have always been those who have crusaded against ignorance, who have insisted on what Friedrich Nietzsche would call a "revaluation of values." In some cases they have been martyred for going against the herd. Theirs is an intellectual, ethical, and social mission all in one. They are gadflies one and all, scions of Socrates.

Friedrich Nietzsche wonders whether it really is more "difficult simply to accept . . . what is considered truth in the circle of one's relatives and of many good men, and what, moreover, really comforts and elevates man," than it is "to strike new paths, fighting the habitual, experiencing the insecurity of independence and the frequent wavering of one's feelings and even one's conscience, proceeding often without any consolation. . . ." Nietzsche suggests that "if you wish to strive for peace of soul and pleasure, then believe; if you wish to be a devotee of truth, then inquire." In this vein, Charles Sanders Peirce, a pioneering American philosopher of science and language in the late nineteenth and early twentieth centuries, wrote that in a sense the "sole rule of reason" is that "in order to learn you must desire to learn, and in so desiring not be satisfied with what you already incline to think." From this rule, Peirce said there "follows one corollary which itself deserves to be inscribed upon every wall of the city of philosophy: Do not block the way of inquiry."

In a modest way, those who take part in Socrates Café are continuing the heretical tradition of the gadfly. What becomes evident in the course of our dialogues is that no one seems yet to have come up with *the* authoritative or definitive answer on any question. All opinions, all so-called truths, are never the last word. But some truths do tend to prevail or hold up better than others after being put through the Socratic wringer.

Laszlo Versenyi puts it this way: "For Socrates, to know something means to be able to give reasons for it, to defend it by rational argument and to demonstrate it to others. It means to hold something . . . as a conclusion fastened by a long chain of reasoning. . . ." Socratic inquiry affords us the opportunity to engage with sharp and passionate minds, to consider great thoughts, to weigh in on the timeless questions and issues. It compels us to give well-supported reasons for why we hold certain philosophies to be tenable and others to be unfounded. What's more, the discovery that even the most astute thinkers often have glaring flaws and blind spots in their philosophies is a constant reminder of the fact that we're all human, all too human.

Christopher
Phillips

THE QUEST FOR HONESTY

Through his inimitable manner of interrogating the Sophists, Socrates revealed that the Sophists' blarney—and expensive blarney at that, since they dispensed it for a pretty penny—wasn't worth much. As then, there are plenty of sophists today, both within and without the confines of academia. The noted contemporary philosopher-scholar Roger Scruton wrote a piercing essay in the Sunday *Times* of London about "the return of the sophist." Scruton tells how today's sophists "no longer . . . guide us towards the truth, through awakening our inherent reasoning powers." Instead, Scruton writes, the new sophist "compares his goods favourably with those of the psychotherapist. . . . He parades before us a catalogue of 'belief systems,' helps us to identify our own among them, and maybe encourages us to replace it with something more up-to-date." And, says Scruton, "in order to persuade the client that her money has been well invested, the favoured 'belief system' will be dressed up in suitable mumbo-jumbo, and priced at a rate that will make it psychologically necessary for the client to persuade herself that she is being cured." Scruton contrasts these new sophists to the timeless example of integrity embodied by Socrates, "whom Plato immortalised in his dialogues" and who "was not a sophist, but a true philosopher" who "awakens the spirit of inquiry" and who enables those with whom he is engaged in dialogue to discover their own answers to life's riddles. The philosopher who exemplifies Socrates, Scruton writes, "is the midwife, and his duty is to help us to be what we are—free and rational beings, who lack nothing that is required to understand our condition. The sophist, by contrast, misleads us with cunning fallacies, takes advantage of our weakness, and offers himself as the solution to problems of which he himself is the cause."

Socrates compared the true philosopher to a physician who helps inoculate men and women against the seductive half-truths of sophists, as well as against bigotry, inhumanity, and propaganda, by teaching them to think carefully, conscientiously, critically—and honestly. In this vein, the type of philosophizing practiced at Socrates Café by the "new Socratics" is not so much a search for absolute truth and certainty as it is a quest for honesty.

The new Socratics know that philosophical inquiry is no panacea or magic bullet for our problems and that it would be the height of dishonesty to portray philosophy in such a light. Indeed, has a problem ever been cured or solved that has not given rise to a host of new ones? It's not simply that this is part and parcel of the experience of being human. Rather, what is called for in the Socratic quest for honesty is the ability to distinguish intractable problems from forward-looking ones whose formulation and exploration enables an inquirer to become more free, more rational, more aware of why she is who she is and how she can be who she aspires to be.

NO PLACE LIKE HOME

Christopher
Phillips

I'm early. I am at a stately housing complex for about three hundred senior citizens that is located near my boyhood hometown in Virginia. I don't quite know what to do with myself, so I linger in the corridor outside the room where we are to meet. It takes me a short while to notice that a small, trim woman with animated hazel eyes is seated nearby on a cushioned bench.

"Are you the philosopher?" she asks me when she sees that I see her.

I don't quite know how to reply. I have trouble with the label "philosopher." I think, "What is a philosopher?" Walter Kaufmann, a modern philosopher who until his death in 1980 at the age of fifty-nine was a professor at Princeton University, compellingly described a philosopher as someone who fights our fears "to understand things that clash with their own customs, privileges, or beliefs" and tries to make us "more sensitive to other points of view, and to show how an outlook that is widely slandered and misunderstood looks and feels from the inside." John Herman Randall, Jr., who was a professor of philosophy at Columbia University for over half a century, said the most essential and creative function of a philosopher is that of a "statesman of ideas" in whom "speculative power—the power to look upon what is—is added to critical acumen—the power to make it all fit together [and] work out a newer and more inclusive idea, which will embrace the warring beliefs, and accord them both intellectual justice." At his "most impressive," a philosopher can give us novel perspectives "on all time and all eternity."

Finally, in reply to the woman's question, I say, "Well, yes, and no."

She laughs. "You're a philosopher all right," she says. She has a German accent.

"Where are you from?" I ask her.

"Well," she says, and then pauses. Now it is her turn to consider how best to respond. Eventually she says, "Until I moved here two months ago to be close to my brother after my husband died, I lived for years in Rome. I was a pediatrician there. But I never thought of it as home."

"Are you from Germany?"

"In a sense" is her enigmatic reply. "I was born there. But I guess the truth is I've never really had a home. I'm not sure there's any such thing as home."

No such thing as home? I don't press her to elaborate right then because it is time for Socrates Café to get under way. The room we gather in is informal, almost homey. It has small round antique tables with bright white cloth covers and comfortable cushioned chairs.

"What is home?" I ask the thirty or so participants, exchanging a knowing look with the woman with whom I was talking before the session began. She simultaneously smiles and frowns at me.

The woman sitting right beside her, who for my benefit is wearing a name tag that says "Mildred," says, "I'll tell you what home *isn't*." Pounding her palms on the chair on which she is sitting, she then says emphatically, "This place is not my home. The only reason I'm here is because this is where my children dumped me. I'd rather be anywhere else but here." She then reminisces a bit about her years in New York. With evident pride, she says she moved there six decades ago, against her family's wishes, to be a social worker. "I left my cozy home in the Midwest by choice and made a new home for myself in the Bronx." She almost beams with pride as she says this. Then her expression seems to darken. She looks around at all of us in the room. "But I am not here by choice. So it can't be home. A home is a place you choose to live."

"Very few of us ever had the luxury of choosing where we live," another resident replies. "I lived where I could find work and provide a good home for my wife and kids."

Another resident then says firmly, "Home is where your bed is. This place is where my bed is. This place is my home."

Mildred calls out, "How many of you feel like this place is your home?"

Only three participants raise their hands, and they do so tentatively. "I must say I'm surprised that so few of you think of this as your home," says the resident who believes home is where your bed is.

"This is one of my homes," says an elegantly dressed woman with lustrous gray hair that falls below her shoulders. "I still have my home in Florida, too."

"Do you come and go between them?" I ask.

"Well, no," she says. She seems almost embarrassed to have to admit this. Then she says, "But I never plan to sell it. As long as I have it, I feel I still have a home there."

She pauses. "What about that expression, 'make yourself at home'?" she then asks. "It makes me ask myself, 'Where are the places I feel at home?' Even though I've been here for several years now, I still don't feel at home. I still feel here like I did when I first moved into my house in Florida so long ago. That first month I was there, it was still just a house. It took time for it to become a home—not just the house but the entire area. But eventually, it became more than a home—it became the place where I learned to cook, where I made lifelong friends, where I fell in love." Then she says wistfully, "I thought I'd eventually come to see this place as a home, but I still haven't. It's still just a house."

"How does a house become a home?" I ask.

"Well," one participant says with a laugh and a sardonic smile, "I think first of all you have to want to live there. Even if there's other places maybe you'd rather be, if you had your druthers, you have to somehow feel that it's your place, your ... base. I just don't feel that way about here, and I don't know if I ever will."

"I don't think I've ever thought of any of the places I've physically lived since becoming an adult as 'home,'" I say. "I think I feel about them as you do about houses. I used to think it was because I moved pretty frequently, but then I think that as a child, I moved frequently too, but very quickly I came to think of whatever place we lived in as a home and not just a house."

After a moment's pause to collect my thoughts, I say, "Sometimes I think the only time I feel at home is when I'm on the road. I was a freelance journalist for many years, so I traveled constantly and I got used to spending most of my nights in motel rooms. To this day, after I'm home for more than a week, I start to get antsy. I pull out the atlas and look at all the places I've been and all the places I'd still like to go."

A demure woman named Audrey who for some time has seemed on the verge of saying something finally says, "I lived most of my adult life in a beautiful apartment on the Upper East Side of Manhattan. It's just occurred to me that all those years I lived there, I never felt like it was home." She is silent for a moment and then says, "I wonder if it's because it was only an apartment instead of a real home. But I don't think of here as a real home either. I wish I understood why...."

"What is a real home?" I ask.

"A *real* home is a place where you knocked and they let you in," says Mildred. Looking at Audrey, she says, "I bet the reason you don't think of the places you lived as homes is because they weren't places you ever chose to live, but places that were chosen for you. Even though they let you in, you never knocked."

"I think you're absolutely right," comes the soft reply.

"A real home is where you were born and raised," says a woman who throughout the discussion has been standing in the doorway, leaning heavily on a cane. For some reason she hasn't or won't come all the way in to join us.

"My childhood home, which is nearby, and which is where my parents still live, doesn't feel much like home to me anymore," I say to her. "My bedroom slowly but surely became an extra room for my mom. In fact, I don't even have a key anymore."

"You can't go home again," a resident laments. While fingering her pearl necklace, she eventually says, "Well, maybe you can. But it's not the same and you're not the same. You can go back, but is it still home? Or is it a new home? Is it a stranger's home?"

The way she has questioned her original view about home reminds me of George Webber, the protagonist in Thomas Wolfe's novel *You Can't Go Home Again*, who said that "the essence of belief is doubt, the essence of reality is questioning." For Webber—whose life often mirrors that of Wolfe himself—home is the place you come from, and the place you leave in order to discover the world beyond and, in the process, break out of your existential eggshell. Years later, Webber returned to his native home after writing a successful novel. But he soon fled when its denizens expressed outrage over his book's scathing social commentary about his hometown. The book's final memorable passage is said to have come from a voice that has spoken to Webber in the night: "To lose the earth you know, for greater knowing; to lose the life you have, for greater life; to leave the friends you loved, for greater loving; to find a land more kind than home, more large than earth." In his lifelong sojourn in far-flung places, Thomas Wolfe himself seemed to have found "a land more kind than home." But he evidently did not consider this land to *be* home. And even though he felt he couldn't go home again, he still felt the home of his youth was home. It was part of the fabric of his being. In a physical and an existential sense, Wolfe felt a rootedness and a connectedness there that no distance in time or place could erase, and that no other land on this planet, no matter how kind, could replace.

After a thoughtful silence, the retired pediatrician says with an air of finality, "Home is where your friends are. My brother is here. And in the two months I've been here I've already made four good friends. And that is enough." She pauses and then says more hesitantly, "So . . . it is becoming home here, sort of."

"Home is where your heart is," Mildred says.

"What does that mean?" I want to know.

"It's where you have pleasant memories," she replies. "It's the place where I learned to ride a bike and to drive a car, the place where I had my first kiss, the place where I go for family reunions, the place to which I make almost all my long-distance phone calls. It's the special place I care about more than any other."

"I come from a broken home," another resident responds. She is perched precariously on the edge of her chair and leans forward with her elbows on her knees and her face pressed between her hands. "I don't have many pleasant memories from there, but it's still home to me. I think it's better to say that home is where you have memories, pleasant or not." She pauses and then says, "But I'm already wondering if even that's correct. I mean, we have memories of lots of things besides home."

"I think memories themselves are a type of home," says a man sitting beside her. "Vladimir Nabokov wrote that 'memory is the only real estate.' Maybe he meant that you can be stripped of everything else you own, but no one can take away your memories."

"My older sister has Alzheimer's, so she has been robbed of her memories, and of her identity," another participant says. Everyone falls silent. He eventually adds, "I really think we're straying too far when we start talking about places besides a physical structure being a home. For instance, my sister lives in a nursing home. Most of the time she doesn't even know exactly where she is, but it's still her home."

"If that's so, then are all the places where we've each lived at one point or another in our lives in some sense 'home'?" I ask.

"No," the pediatrician says, shaking her head. "I was born and raised in Germany. It was my homeland, but it is in no way a home to me." She relates that she and her family had to leave Germany to escape the horrific Nazi persecution of the Jews. From there she went to Italy. "Germany in no sense is or was my home," she says.

"But your roots are in Germany," one woman says to her.

"It's *not* my home," she replies firmly, and falls silent.

"Even though it seems that all of us have at least a somewhat different idea of what home is and where our home is," I say, "is there some sort of connecting thread for the concept of home that we all share?"

A woman sitting beside me says with hardly a moment's pause, "It seems that home is a place, a special place, where we each in a certain sense reside. For many of us this place can be nice and comforting, for others it can be rather awful and discomforting. But in all instances it's still home."

"I think you're right," says a whisper-thin man. He has been silent until now. He then says, "Whenever there was a war near our home, we moved. During my childhood years, to escape the Bolshevik Revolution, we moved from Russia to Canada. We then eventually moved to Hawaii, then to the mainland of the U.S. when World War II broke out. I know that some here are uncomfortable with this view, but my home was not a house. My home was my family. My home was the people I loved most."

"I'm the only family I've ever had," another participant says softly. The severely stooped man clutches the black cane that lies across his legs. "I was raised in an orphanage. It wasn't a pleasant experience, and I never considered it home. After I left the orphanage, I lived by myself and relied only on myself—until now, when I have no choice but to accept help from the staff here at this residence. But like the woman said at the beginning of this conversation, this is not my home." Then he thumps his chest and says, "*I* am my home."

There is a considerable lull. Finally the man who spoke before him says, "Since this discussion is called Socrates Café, I've been thinking about Socrates. And I think, for Socrates, home was all of Athens. And that's one reason why, when the tribunal who prosecuted him gave him a choice of being exiled from Athens instead of being put to death, he refused. Because to go out from Athens would've made him feel homeless. He preferred death to homelessness."

He looks at the pediatrician. "Germany is only where your roots are. Like you said, home is where the people you love are."

This moves me to say, "The one and only time I went with my mom to the coal mining camp in West Virginia where she was born, I said to her, 'So this is your home.' And she replied, 'This is where my roots are, but you are my home."

"Did your mom always make you feel at home asking questions?" the retired pediatrician then asks me.

"She sure did," I tell her.

She asks me to tell them more about my mom and where she is from. "The coal mining camp where she was born and raised is still standing, still intact, though it's a ghost town," I say. "Since that first time I went there with my mom, I drive there whenever

I can. I try to imagine how my mom, in this oppressive environment, was able to so much as imagine that there was any other world, or any other possibilities for herself.

"Somehow, with little encouragement from anyone else, my mom developed a love for the written word. She would sneak away to the little library built by the coal baron at every opportunity and read every book she could get her hands on. By reading, she began to discover the world that lay beyond the mountains, and she began to discover the universe in her mind. I don't think I've ever met a more gifted critical thinker than my mom.

Christopher Phillips

"Even when I was a child, instead of telling me the answer," I go on, "my mom pushed me to develop my own belief system, to discover my own way, my own truths, by my own lights. I was a relentless interrogator who peppered her with question after question. But she never replied, 'Just because, that's why.' She never was the least bit exasperated by my bottomless well of questions. In fact, she seemed to enjoy every single question I asked. Whether I asked, 'Why is the sky blue?' or 'Why is there a sky?' or 'Why are there questions?' her first response typically was 'Why do you think . . . the sky is blue, there is a sky, there are questions?' And from that starting point, we'd have a dialogue. She challenged and pushed me to discover my own answers."

"It sounds like your mom is a big reason why you're doing what you're doing now," Mildred says.

"I think so, absolutely," I reply. "The more I think about it, the more it seems like it was only a matter of time before I would have to start something like Socrates Café."

"Just like Socrates," Mildred says, "you feel most at home when you're philosophizing with people anywhere and everywhere who want to philosophize with you."

She smiles and says, "Don't you think Socrates Café is your home?"

HOMEWARD BOUND

Is where I am, for all intents and purposes, who I am? Is my home one I carry with me, my way of being in the world? Are my world and my worldview one and the same? What if I said *where I am* is *who I am*? Would that seem outlandish? Is the *where* consistent with the *who*?

At times I feel about my home the way Mark Twain did about his house in Hartford, Connecticut, where he wrote: "Our house ... had a heart, and a soul, and eyes to see us with; and approvals and solicitudes and deep sympathies; it was of us, and we were in its confidence, and lived in its grace and in the peace of its benediction." At other times my sense of home is more like writer Jim Morgan's when he wrote in *If These Walls Had Ears: The Biography of a House* that "the story of America has always been the story of a search for home. It's a restless journey in which we never seem to arrive."

FREE AT LAST

At a Socrates Café in San Francisco held on National Secretaries' Day, a somewhat harried-looking woman sits silently while I ask for questions. Like someone who is dying to propose a question but at the same time is afraid to ask, she keeps raising her hand halfway in the air, then jerking it back down just as I look her way.

"Do you have a question?" I ask her.

"No," she replies while her head protests, nodding up and down.

"I think you have a question," I say.

"Well," she replies, "I guess I do. But I don't know if it's appropriate for a philosophical discussion."

"I bet it is," I say.

Christopher
Phillips

That does the trick. She blurts out, "How can a sensitive, intelligent person get stuck in a lousy job?" It seems a catharsis of sorts for her to have purged herself of this question. It turns out this newcomer to the gathering is a secretary for an investment banker.

She goes on to say, "I work in a cubicle with no windows in a nice-paying job with no future. I want so much more out of my working life." She sighs. "But here I am, stuck."

"Isn't the human condition one of stuckness?" says a slight, swarthy man with shoulder-length coarse hair and an usually deep voice. "I'm stuck in this body. I'm stuck with and in the mind I have. I'm stuck in this universe. I'm stuck with breathing if I want to keep living. So I'm stuck all around."

"Sounds like we should start out by examining our 'philosophies of stuckness,'" I say, all the while thinking that one of the most vexing issues in the entire history of philosophy has been that of whether we are free to do as we please, or whether our actions are largely determined by factors and circumstances beyond our control. One intriguing view on this issue is that of the Dutch-born philosopher Baruch Spinoza, who maintained that a human being isn't constrained by outside forces, but rather is "determined" by forces and conditions arising from her own nature. Spinoza felt that this was actually a type of freedom, which he called "self-determination." He meant by this that our physical and mental makeup "joins forces" with our past development and our present relationship to the world around us to determine the course we chart in our lives. For these views, he was expelled in 1656 from the Jewish community in Amsterdam as a heretic.

"I think there's good stuck and bad stuck," says the woman with the yucky job. "And I feel like I'm bad stuck. And my job is the culprit for it. If I liked my job, I wouldn't mind so much the other areas of stuckness—breathing, my body, my mind, the universe, what have you."

A man who has been standing by the entrance to the café for quite some time, as if undecided whether he wants to take part, now joins the discussion. He says he works for a pittance as a freelance graphic designer for what he calls "socially conscious nonprofit groups." He goes on to say, "Following what these two have been saying, even if you have a job you love, you're still 'stuck,' in a sense. Because you're still imprisoned in the workaday world. Even if you love your job, maybe, if you had your druthers, you wouldn't work at all. But you can't not work, unless maybe you're filthy rich—and even the filthy rich probably have to work at least a little bit at staying filthy rich. So you're stuck, trapped, in a prison of sorts, even if it's a prison you love."

A rotund man, his breathing so loud and labored that at times it distracts me from the dialogue, has just ordered his second carafe of wine. Now he says, "Life is a job."

"Life is a job," I repeat, and press further. "Which I guess means, among other things, that the business of living itself requires work of a sort, which makes it a job of a sort."

"But even as an adage, life's not only a job, at its best, is it?" I go on. "Or at least, aren't there all kinds of jobs—and can't we characterize them as everything from terrible to wonderful, and many things in between, based at least in part on the kinds of work they require us to do? At its best, can't a job be a form of self-expression, requiring us to work in a way that, far from being a drag, is fulfilling? Can't the right kinds of jobs represent a form of stuckness that can actually help us to be *freer*?"

The bequeather of the truism does not respond. He pretends

to be fully absorbed in pouring his next glass of wine. He appears to have wanted to spew forth his adage without being subjected to subsequent critique or comment of any sort.

I turn to the secretary. "Maybe," I say, "the job you're stuck in can be what motivates you to seek a job that is more self-fulfilling. Emerson said a person is relieved and gay when he has put his heart into his work and done his best. I think it would make more sense to say something like, a person should put his heart into finding the type of work that'll inspire her to give it everything she's got. And it may take quite a circuitous route to discover work like that. In my case, if I hadn't been stuck in a number of jobs that ranged from what I'd call lousy to not-so-lousy, to somewhat rewarding but still not good enough, I doubt I'd ever eventually have hit upon what I'm doing now—which for me is the ideal job. All these other jobs compelled me to work hard to discover more fully who I want to be."

"The best I've been able to figure," the graphic designer chimes in, "is: Try to find something that you love so much that you would do it for free. Now, I'm sure that the first thing that comes to mind when you first hear someone say something like this is 'It sure sounds nice on paper. But it isn't practical.' Wrong! It *is* practical. Because if you don't find that job that feeds your passion, that makes you excited to get up in the morning and give everything you have to your work, then what are you left with?"

Another participant says, "It seems like in certain ways your existence is much less worthwhile than it could be if you don't take well-calculated risks and do what you really want to with your work life. I have so many acquaintances who make loads of money, but their spirit is dead. They're like the living dead. So money isn't the answer when it comes to finding work that you don't mind being 'stuck' in."

I notice that the woman who initially posed the question has been scribbling furiously, as if taking down every word the graphic designer has said. She stops abruptly, clicks her pen as furiously as she had been scribbling a moment before, and looks up. "I recently read Hannah Arendt's *The Human Condition*," she says. "I've been haunted by one thing she wrote. I think I'm quoting this right: 'The task and potential greatness of mortals lie in their ability to produce things—works and deeds and words—which would deserve to be at home in everlastingness.' I guess I've been trying to discover what deed I want to do, and what deed I can do, that will deserve a home in everlastingness. I mean, I think we all have some unique ability that we can transform into our life's work and passion. At least, it's what I *choose* to believe. And yet, because I choose to believe this, I get very frustrated when I feel, like I do too much of the time, that I'm not putting all my energies toward something that will put my imprint on the world and will in some way be everlasting."

She stays quiet for quite some time. "You know," she then says as she tucks her pen and notepad in her purse, "I've been actively involved in community theater for almost a decade. The founder of the group has asked me several times over the years if I wanted to be involved full-time. He offered me way less than half the pay and said I'd work nearly a third more hours than I do in my current job. But it'd be work I really enjoy. Work I consider play. And work that I consider, for myself, timeless, because I believe that good theater has the capacity to help us see the world and ourselves in new ways.

"But I've never taken his offer seriously. It's not just because I've been scared. And it's not really that I'm all that hesitant to live more frugally. I think it's mainly because I've never seen it as *work*. I've always had this prejudice that if I didn't up and move to New York and try to become a famous actress—a star—then I should never try to make money in this field. I've always looked at my community theater work as a 'hobby,' because I convinced myself it was never appropriate to settle for something so 'low' in the world of acting as that kind of work." She slaps her forehead and says, "What a horrible prejudice I've had!" She says this last sentence so loud that a number of participants are startled out of whatever reverie they were in. "Community theater is my love and passion. I have no interest at all in moving from here to New York and trying to become a famous actress. I want my life's work to be my involvement in community theater."

To my surprise, she stands up. "I'm gonna go for it!" she proclaims. I almost think she is going to run from the room and go straight to her investment banker boss, tell him she quits, and then scoot directly to the community theater group. But then she seems to realize that it is 10 P.M., too late to make much more headway tonight. Still standing, she looks around at us, wondering if she has anything to be embarrassed about. She sits back down, smooths the folds in her dress, and then, in her best Scarlett O'Hara impersonation, says, "After all, tomorrow is another day!"

BROTHER, CAN YOU SPARE A CELL?

Where am I stuck?

Is this another way of asking, What, if anything, are my prisons?

What if you're in a prison from which you don't want to escape?

Jean-Paul Sartre, the famous existentialist philosopher, novelist, playwright, and social critic, maintained in *Being and Nothingness* that we are "condemned to be free." Sartre believed the lot of humankind to be one of limitless freedom. A witness to the tragedies of World War II (Sartre himself was briefly captured by the Germans), he surely knew of the many obstacles to human freedom; nonetheless, he felt that as conscious beings, we are always free to try to change our situation. He wrote that we are "thrown" into a world that has no rules or structure other than those which we choose to give it. There are people who "want to be massive and impenetrable" and who "never seek but that which one has already found." But according to Sartre, those with the temerity to shun convention and make free choices in their search for self are "authentic," while those who conform to roles dictated by society and recoil at their unfettered freedom are practicing "bad faith."

One of my best friends, in his mid-forties, longs to travel, to be a writer and photographer, to learn languages. "Why don't you seize the day and go for it?" I exhort him.

"I can't," he says. He shrugs. "Hey, my life is over."

What unnerves me the most is the look on his face when he says this. It is not one of despair or disappointment or even resignation. It is a look of relief. He seems to take pleasure in convincing himself that he can't move one centimeter forward in the direction of his dreams.

He is the picture of health, financially secure, extremely intelligent. Yet he has erected a prison for himself. I try gently to chip away at it. I tell him that it's not too late to realize his dreams, that, for instance, Alex Haley, the author of *Roots*, didn't even make the attempt to become a professional writer until middle age, when he had retired from the Coast Guard. He looks at me with a blank expression. I think he knows what I'm trying to get across to him, but he doesn't want to let it seep in. He's built an impermeable, albeit invisible, barrier around himself. He'd rather stay with the "my life is over" spiel. I try to give him a "get out of jail free" card. But nothing doing. He prefers his all-too-comfy, custom-made prison.

Sitting in a cell nearby is another friend of mine, a lawyer in West Virginia. He's an excellent lawyer and at a young age has already made quite a name for himself in his neck of the woods. The problem is, as he's confided to me on a number of occasions, he hates being a lawyer. He wants to quit his despised profession and become an anthropology professor. He is still young, single, debt-free. "What's stopping you?" I ask.

"I'm locked in," he laments, swishing the swivel stick within his tumbler of bourbon on the rocks. "In two more years I'll be vested. I'll be a partner."

"But . . . you don't want to be a lawyer," I say. "Why spend two more years in the firm until you're vested? By then you'll be locked in even more."

He studies me. He takes a good long swallow of his bourbon. He puts his tumbler down and he looks somewhere past my shoulder. His lips are moving. He seems to be having a conversation with himself. Finally he looks at me and says, "Do you think I'm crazy?"

I look at him quizzically.

"I'd be crazy to leave at this point and start all over again." His angry eyes are tearing.

Part of his job is to represent the city in prosecuting criminals. He has an exceptionally high conviction rate. He's so good that he's even managed to convict himself, to a life he despises, without parole.

Can your emotions be prisons?

Many modern philosophers think it's a commonplace that emotion is the opposite of reason and hinders a person's ability to be objective. Søren Kierkegaard argued that, to the contrary, the most insightful knowledge springs from, and is the fruit of, an intense and impassioned emotional outpouring.

But some emotions can be paralyzing and debilitating. Walter Kaufmann noted that you can live in the grip of resentment, jealousy, hate, fear, or grief, and that to this day many deem it virtually impossible to transcend such emotions. "Yet philosophers have long recognized that this widespread notion is false," Kaufmann wrote, "and Socrates, the Stoics and Epicureans, and Spinoza are among those who have tried to teach humanity how to emancipate itself from this bondage" through self-understanding, which Kaufmann says is "self-transcendence. . . . It changes one's life." But I think there are many types of self-understanding, and not all of them are of the liberating type that leads a person to make positive life changes. You may understand why you are oppressed, why you have paralyzing fears, why you habitually procrastinate; but if you don't know how to go about improving your circumstances, then the self-understanding you've gained may lead you to feel more in bondage, more paralyzed by fear or oppression, than ever.

In all fairness to Kaufmann, I think the self-understanding of which he speaks is an emancipating type. Consider the method of questioning he espouses in order to overcome such debilitating emotions as resentment, which is one of the most constricting prisons:

> One can ask oneself for a start: Am I free of resentment? And if not, what do I resent? What precisely? And how rational is it that I . . . resent this but not that? Never mind at that point whether you think that you can let go. Just ask yourself whether you might be better off if you did, and whether you would like yourself better. Think of alternatives, using your imagination.

You need no analyst to do that; you can do it though it is not at all easy. What is then harder, of course, is then going on to shed resentment . . . ; but that, too, can be done even if it should take some time.

Christopher
Phillips
Kaufmann's method of questioning doesn't leave you dangling after you answer some aspect of "Who am I?" but requires that you "think of alternatives, using your imagination," and then commit to changing those aspects of yourself that keep you from being the person you aspire to be.

Richard Tarnas wrote that Socrates, through his words and deeds, "embodied an abiding conviction that the act of rational self-criticism could free the human mind from the bondage of false opinion." The method Socrates used to set his mind free is available to anyone, at anytime, in any place.

You may want to ask yourself sometime: What are my prisons? Are some of my prisons good and even necessary? Are others constricting and even debilitating? Are there ways to fortify the good prisons while at the same time ridding myself of others?

What kind of place is a prison—of the federal type?

Immanuel Kant strongly endorsed the prison system and the penalization of criminals. For instance, Kant said reason dictated that thieves be sentenced to forced labor in prisons: "A person who steals makes everybody else's property insecure; so in effect he ends up robbing himself . . . of the security of all possible property; he does not have anything and cannot acquire anything, but he still wants to live, though this is not possible unless others feed him. But since the state will not do this for nothing, he has to put his powers at the disposal of the state for whatever labor it deems fit. . . ."

Nearly a century later, the French philosopher, historian, and social critic Michel Foucault, in *Discipline and Punish: The Birth of the Prison*, maintained that prisons only serve to harden and perfect the professional criminal. Foucault challenged the widely held assumption that the advent of the prison system was a progressive and humane development. He argued that, to the contrary, it was a disturbing sign of increasing social and political control. Foucault said that the purpose of modern penitentiaries was similar to that of modern asylums—namely, to separate "abnormal" or "deviant" individuals from the so-called normal ones within society at large. Foucault further asserted that modern society, in which rigid regimentation and conformity are cardinal virtues, was itself becoming more and more like a prison. "Is it surprising that . . . factories, schools, barracks, hospitals . . . all resemble prisons?" he asked.

Unlike Kant, Foucault studied comprehensively the actual conditions in prisons and juxtaposed his account with his considered perspective on the state of society. Only then did he come to his reasoned conclusions about both prisons and society. Nonetheless, as compelling as I and countless others might find his insights, they are no more the last word than are Kant's. Though Foucault's conclusions may well hold true in many or even most cases, I do not think they are universally true. I think there are many individual exceptions that have shown that prisons can be, among many other things, liberating places.

The Austrian-born philosopher Ludwig Wittgenstein is said to have used the time he spent in an Italian prison camp during World War I to develop more fully his thoughts on the foundations of logic and mathematics and complete his *Tractatus Logico-Philosophicus*. It turned out to be the only work published in his lifetime, and it precipitated a revolution in philosophy. This landmark work, which emphasized the importance of the study of language, led to his becoming one of the most influential

Christopher
Phillips

philosophers of the century and to the development of several important fields of philosophy: logical positivism, which applies the principles of logic, mathematics, and empirical science to virtually every field of thought; linguistic analysis, which aims to examine and clarify the many uses of language; and semantics, the study of the meaning of words, and the relationship of signs to the objects they denote.

The stories are legion about people who have taken advantage of the time they spent behind bars to free their minds, escaping from the mental shackles that in turn, upon their release from prison, enabled them to escape their harsh environment.

The civil rights leader Malcolm X, for instance, emerged from his time spent in prison, where he converted to the Muslim faith, a changed man—in many ways a *new* man. He had nurtured almost incomparable critical and creative thinking skills from his disciplined and voluminous reading while behind bars. In his autobiography, he recounts how he poured over countless works of philosophy and came to conclude that "most Occidental philosophy had largely been borrowed from the Oriental thinkers. Socrates, for instance, traveled in Egypt. . . . Obviously [he] got some of his wisdom from the East's wise men."

In prison, he literally transcended his former self and became for me and countless others a paradigm of an autonomous person who succeeded in bridging racial and cultural divides. He was the epitome of a person who managed to free himself of very justifiable resentment—one of the most rigid and confining prisons of all—to realize his aspirations. What he accomplished is even more admirable when one considers that from the first moment he was brought into this world, he faced inordinately oppressive circumstances, and was raised in the midst of a society that bred and fomented inequality and racial animosity. Just as he learned from reading about the lives of those who had made dramatic self-transformations, by his example, Malcolm X in his own right became a beacon to all who believe that you change the world by changing yourself. Few people seem to have completely freed themselves of resentment—one of the most constraining prisons of all—as Malcolm X.

In later years, he said he "often reflected on the new vistas that reading opened to me. I knew right there in prison that reading had changed forever the course of my life. As I see it today, the ability to read awoke inside me some long dormant craving to be mentally alive." To be sure, he couldn't know everything, didn't learn everything, before he was assassinated. But he was forever open to new opportunities to learn and think and question in new ways, and like few others, he took for his own the difficult and exhilarating and unending challenge of setting himself free.

We might let him inspire us to break out of an endless series of cells.

A WISE PLACE

It is late afternoon and raining heavily as I arrive at a medium-security prison in Northern California. The old and unadorned yellow brick facility is wedged in a narrow valley on the outskirts of a congested suburb. I pass through a number of checkpoints at the prison before I finally enter the large gymnasium-like room where I am to facilitate Socrates Café. The prison official who arranged for my visit is there to greet me. She had earlier told me that about twenty inmates would take part. That seemed to me an ideal size. But she now tells me that sixty inmates are inside waiting for Socrates Café to get under way. I have to struggle to quell the anxiety welling up inside me. Would I be able to facilitate a worthwhile dialogue with so many taking part? Should I just turn tail and bolt out of there? It had taken months to get permission to hold a Socrates Café with the prisoners. It had taken letters and phone calls and finally a meeting with prison officials, and at last a firm date was scheduled. I can't leave now.

But I wonder whether this will be an exercise in futility. A friend who'd once held "group dynamics" discussions with inmates had told me it was his experience that they wouldn't reveal anything intimate about themselves because of fears they'd lose face or lose their stature with their fellow inmates. "They'll never engage in the kind of discussion you hold in the outside world" was his pessimistic prognosis.

When I walk into the meeting room, an inmate, a burly man with a craggy and careworn face, comes up to me and says, "What's the weather like out there?"

"It's pretty miserable," I tell him.

"I'd still rather be out there than in here," he says, and sort of smiles.

"My name's Wolf," he says. We shake hands. Then he says, "Have you ever heard that saying, 'Man is a wolf to man'?"

I say I have. "I don't think that's true," he says. "I think that saying gives wolves a bad rap. If man hurts his fellow man, we shouldn't go around saying that he acts like a wolf. Wolves are noble animals, unlike man."

Then a very tall, striking black man with a neatly trimmed beard and a piercing gaze introduces himself. His name is John. He obviously wants to ask me something but he seems shy, hesitant. Finally he says, "I hope this doesn't sound stupid, but I was wondering . . ." He pauses some more, as if thinking how best to say what he wants to say. Then he asks, "Isn't philosophy really the study of 'why?'"

"That sounds like a wonderful definition of philosophy," I reply.

All of the other inmates—garbed in loose-fitting pajama-like orange pants, short-sleeved shirts and slippers—are already seated on metal stools along a number of large rectangular benches. The benches and stools are bolted to the floor, a precautionary measure to keep the inmates from throwing the seats and benches at one another. Armed guards are stationed all around the perimeter of the high-ceilinged, windowless room.

Most inmates are drinking coffee. A few have their heads down on the table and seem asleep. But most seem at least a little curious about what is about to take place. I wonder how I can keep the conversation from becoming unwieldy, how I can further this quest of mine to better enable me and others, wherever and whoever they might be, to seek Socrates. I am introduced to the inmates as "a philosophy teacher." I quickly correct that. "I'm a philosopher, and I do facilitate philosophy discussions," I say to the group, "but I don't consider myself a teacher in the traditional sense of the word. I have every expectation at every Socrates Café that I'll learn much more from the other participants than they could ever learn from me."

I then talk a little bit about how I felt that I'd lived certain stretches of my adult life in a kind of intellectual and emotional wasteland. I talk about how at a certain crossroads in my life I'd been moved by the words of Socrates that "the unexamined life is not worth living," and how my renewed "communion" with Socrates reawakened and rekindled my sense of the possibilities of "applying" the method of philosophical inquiry practiced by Socrates in my life and perhaps in the lives of others. I don't seem to know how to quit talking. I don't even seem to know why I'm saying what I'm saying. Fortunately an inmate raises his hand to interrupt me. It is Wolf. "What does philosophy mean?" he asks.

"The original Hellenistic Greek word for philosophy, *philosophia*, translates into 'love of wisdom,'" I say.

"What is wisdom?" he asks.

"What do you take it to mean?" I reply.

"I think you can only answer this by answering what a wise person is," one says.

"So, what is a wise person?" I ask.

He does not reply for quite some time. Finally he says, "I think a wise person is someone who has the rare ability to apply effectively what he's learned about life and about people. He's not easily misled and he doesn't mislead."

Another says, "A wise person knows how to apply his knowledge through experience. And he's someone who shares with others what he knows."

An inmate with a dour expression says, "A wise person is someone who knows what type of knowledge he should share, and what type he shouldn't share. For instance, a man who knows how to defraud an ATM machine wouldn't pass that know-how to someone else if he were wise, because that is a 'bad' kind of knowledge."

Seated on a bench to the left of me, an inmate who so far has been nodding in agreement to everything everyone has said now says, "I'd never thought about it that way before. I'd always thought that a wise person shares everything he knows. But now I think that it isn't wise to share all knowledge."

Then he says, "Do you think there's such a thing as 'bad' wisdom, as opposed to 'good wisdom'?"

Wolf interjects, "There's only good wisdom. 'Bad wisdom' is a contradiction in terms."

A professorial-looking man says in a rather haughty way, "I agree that wisdom can only be good. In Plato's *Laws*, wisdom is considered one of the four virtues, along with temperance, courage, and justice. But in his *Republic*, it's considered the ruling virtue that subsumes the others. Aristotle, on the other hand, made the distinction in his *Politics* between philosophical wisdom and practical wisdom. He wrote that practical wisdom is concerned with 'things human and things about which it is possible to deliberate.' But he said pre-Socratic philosophers like Thales and Anaxagoras only had philosophical wisdom, because they were 'ignorant of what is to their own advantage' and only 'know things that are remarkable, admirable, difficult and divine . . . but useless.'" The fiftyish-looking man with a salt-and-pepper beard and thick glasses then says, without prompting, that he is serving a fifteen-year sentence for embezzling over one hundred thousand dollars from the private college where he used to be an administrator. Many moons earlier, he tells us, he'd earned bachelor's and master's degrees in philosophy from an Ivy League university.

No one else responds. Eventually I say, "Speaking of Aristotle, he was one of the first philosophers to make the observation that 'man is born possessing weapons for the use of wisdom and excellence, which it is possible to employ entirely for the opposite ends.'"

I go on, "Can't wise people do unwise things? Can't we be wise in some areas but absolutely idiotic in others?"

"I think I'm living proof of that," the erstwhile college administrator responds.

"Wisdom is something you strive for but never attain," John then says. But then he quickly adds, "No, that's not quite it. I mean, I think you can attain wisdom, but you can never attain *absolute* wisdom. The wisest people know they can never become but so wise. But even so they keep striving to becoming wiser every day. They strive to strike a better balance between common sense and knowledge and understanding. And they freely share what they've learned—when they think it's beneficial—with others."

"I don't think that knowledge is or even should be shared freely, even if it's beneficial," says the person sitting beside him. "Sometimes you have to pay to learn, you have to earn learning. You have to take classes, you have to buy books and tapes, to gain knowledge, to become wise."

"Socrates never charged anyone to 'learn' from him," Wolf points out. "He preferred to remain poor than to capitalize on his method of wisdom."

"But that doesn't contradict my point," the man insists. "Learning is hard work, it seems to me. You do have to 'pay' for it, 'earn' it—maybe not with money, but with the effort you spend and exert on learning just about anything."

"What do you think is the best way, or some of the best kinds of ways, to learn?" I ask.

"Someone said King Solomon was wise because he spoke in parables," John says. "He wrote so you could learn from the story if you chose to, but he didn't try to cram lessons down your throat. That's 'the wisdom of Solomon.' That's why I like parables, because they respect the intelligence of the reader. They make you feel like you learned something on your own, and they teach us that there's rarely any sort of 'once and for all' type of answer to any significant question."

"I think that's why Søren Kierkegaard used parables—because the meaning you grasped from them was your own, a 'truth' you grasped as meaningful for yourself," says the former college administrator.

"How do you think people become wise?" I ask eventually.

"I know a few people who seem wise beyond their years," a wiry but athletically built man says, "but in general I think a person becomes wise by learning from years of accumulated experiences."

"I think all people are wise," another says.

I ask him, "Do all people learn from their experiences?"

"No," he says.

"Do you think wise people usually learn from their experiences?"

"Yes."

"Then how can all people be wise?"

"I think all people are born wise," he says. "But if we choose not to learn from our experiences, we become less and less wise. I knew better than to use drugs. I knew better than to steal things so I'd have money to buy drugs. I'd been caught before and been in prison before. But I did it again anyway. So I've become less wise as I've gotten older."

"I agree with him," says another. "It's like, one person will touch a pan of hot water once and burn his finger and never do it again. But another will touch it again and again and never seem to learn his lesson."

"I've been in and out of drug treatment programs and prisons, and still I made the same mistakes over and over," says a youngish man with a ragged countenance, his hair dyed in black and yellow streaks. "But this time I really think I've learned my lesson. Because this time I'm ready to learn and I'm ready to be receptive to what others are trying to teach me. So this time it's sinking in, while in the past it came across to me as just a lot of technical words and bullshit that went in one ear and out the other."

A reed-thin man with dark bags under his large green eyes runs his hand through his close-cropped hair and says, "Now that I'm clean of drugs, the fact that I've done drugs in my life gives me an edge over others. Because I know what it's like to have done drugs, I have an experience that many don't have. So this makes me wiser. I hope I never repeat this experience, but it's good that I've had it. It's good to experience 'bad things,' just to have that experience once."

"I disagree with all my heart," says the man who'd just spoken of his revolving-door entry and exit from one drug treatment program and prison after another. "I don't think it was a good experience being a drug addict. I wish to God I'd never tried drugs even once. I wished I'd listened to those who tried to warn me off even trying them. I think if we all thought this philosophy of 'experiencing bad things once' was a good idea, just about everyone in society would be in jail or dead."

"I hear you, man," says the inmate who'd prompted this comment. "But I do think that because I have experienced being a drug addict, and have been able to overcome it, I'll be able to be a much more effective drug abuse counselor once I'm out of prison than I'd've been if I'd never been an addict."

"But what if you hadn't been able to break the addiction?" the other inmate says. "What if you'd ended up dying of an overdose? It's not always possible to overcome these bad things. And what if the bad thing you tried, even just once, didn't just harm you, but others? What if the bad thing you tried was murder?"

The reed-thin inmate smiles at his interrogator. "You've got me there."

Again, there is a comfortable silence as we think over all that's been said so far.

"Who are some of the people you think of as wise?" I eventually ask. "Maybe that'll help us find out what the criteria of wisdom are."

"Gandhi and Martin Luther King, Jr., were wise," says a man with a crescent-shaped scar on one cheek, which if anything heightens his dashing looks. "They practiced and preached nonviolence while trying to bring about social change, and they practiced what they preached. They sacrificed their lives to be an example to others that sometimes you have to be willing to die to set the rest of the world free."

A Mexican man says Pancho Villa was wise. "Even though he was outgunned and outmanned, Villa still managed to defeat the gringo army."

"Does that mean he was wise, or does it just mean he was able to outsmart his opponent?" someone asks him.

"Well, I think being smart enough to defeat a much more powerful opponent who wants to destroy your people requires what I'd call a very shrewd wisdom," he replies.

"Sigmund Freud was wise," a pensive inmate then says. "I learned more from his books than from anyone else about the roots of my own problems. Take his *Interpretation of Dreams*, where he's discussing Hamlet's behavior. He says that all explanations of why we are the way we are are 'capable of interpretation and actually demand nothing less for full understanding.' This is an incredible insight. Freud means that there's not just one irreducible explanation that points to why we are the way we are. Instead, there's numerous explanations, many of which may conflict with one another, but all of which shed light on our selves. It doesn't mean that every explanation is legitimate or revealing, but it does mean that we have to try to understand ourselves from all kinds of standpoints."

Then an inmate who looks to be around nineteen says softly, "My grandfather was wise. If I'd only listened to him, I wouldn't be in jail today."

"I don't think we should only speak about wise people," another says. "We should also speak of wise places. The Grand Canyon is a wise place. Whenever I've been there, in the middle of all that solitude, I've been able to think wise thoughts. Those thoughts come from that wise place."

"What do you mean by 'wise thoughts'?" someone asks him.

"I mean, thoughts that put me at peace," he replies. "Thoughts that make me realize I'm a foibled and flawed person, but that I can always strive to do better, to be better, and that it's my duty to do and be better. Thoughts that make me realize it's okay to follow my own drummer. If I could have taken these thoughts with me away from the Grand Canyon and applied them when I was back in the inner city, I wouldn't be here right now."

"I think Mother Earth herself is a wise place," another says. "She's survived for billions of years, even though we've tried our best to destroy her. She'll still be here long after we're gone."

"But in order for something to be wise, doesn't it have to be conscious?" someone asks him.

"Well, I don't know about you, but I think this earth is conscious," he replies. He's not the only one: in 1979 Dr. James Lovelock, a British chemist, first set forth his Gaia Hypothesis, in which he asserted that the earth should be seen holistically as a "self-regulating living system." According to Lovelock, "The entire range of living matter on Earth, from whales to viruses and from oaks to algae, could be regarded as constituting a single living entity . . . endowed with faculties and powers far beyond those of its constituent parts." If this is so, it would follow that since humans are conscious, and since humans are no more or less than constituent parts of the earth as a whole, then the earth itself is conscious.

"Let's go back to talking about wisdom as it relates to people," I say to the group. "Do you think a wise person would ever say he or she is wise?"

A clean-cut, preppie-looking man sitting on the bench closest to the entrance says, "Didn't Socrates say something like 'The wisest people know they're not very wise'?" He has had his head down for the entire conversation, until now. I had long since assumed that he was fast asleep.

"Can you expand on that?" I ask.

"Plato wrote in his *Apology* that it was Socrates' mission to search out people who his city brothers thought were the wisest of all. He wanted to find out if these people really lived up to their billing. Each time, he came to the same conclusion: They weren't wise. In fact they were fucking idiots." A lot of us laugh. But his expression remains serious.

Then he says, "Hold on a sec." He pulls out an old slender paperback edition of Plato's *Apology* that had been stuffed in his back pocket. As he thumbs through the pages before landing on the one he's looking for, he says, "In the *Apology*, Socrates tells how he cross-examined one guy who was considered by the Athenian bigwigs to be the wisest of the wise and who agreed with their assessment."

He finds the page he's looking for. He clears his throat. "Socrates says here, 'I decided that although the man seemed to many people, and above all to himself, to be wise, in reality he was not wise. I tried to demonstrate to him that he thought he was wise, but actually was not, and as a result I made an enemy of him, and of many of those present [here at the trial]. To myself, as I left him, I reflected: 'Here is one man less wise than me. In all probability neither of us knows anything worth knowing; but he thinks he knows when he doesn't, whereas I, given that I don't in fact know, am at least aware I don't know. Apparently, therefore, I am wiser than him in just this one small detail, that when I don't know something, I don't think I know it either.' From him I went to another man, one of those who seemed wiser than the first. I came to exactly the same conclusion, and made an enemy of him and of many others besides.'"

He raises his head and looks at us. "Socrates showed that the knowledge of these so-called wise men was just a house of cards."

"But unlike those people Socrates came up against, I think the people we've been talking about today are very wise," John says. "If anyone ever asked them if they were wise and they said they weren't, they'd be lying."

"I think what Socrates is saying is that wise people have more humility about their wisdom than most people," replies the man who just read from Plato's *Apology*. I later found out that this man is serving a long sentence for committing grand larceny; this is the fourth time he's been caught and convicted of a felony offense.

"Socrates believed that wise people know that what they know may not be the truth for all time," he goes on to say. "But his judges and persecutors felt that this belief was blasphemy. And you know what? It was. It was good blasphemy. But they didn't want to deal with that, so they decided to kill him."

Thumbing through the pages of his book distractedly, he then says, "And you know what else? If they hadn't passed that evil and idiotic death sentence on Socrates, I bet his wisdom and moral courage wouldn't have stood out so clearly. I bet it wouldn't have stood the test of time and been an inspiration ever since."

To be sure, I was in a prison. I could feel the dull and oppressive sense of confinement all around. But I could also feel that its inhabitants exuded an unusual and even exuberant wisdom. These men engaged in our dialogue with probing and incisive honesty. And while I know that what I am thinking just now may not be a truth for all time, it does occur to me that in many ways they are free. Certainly more free than many with whom I philosophize in the so-called outside world and who seem to live in rigid intellectual prisons of their own making. Even a prison can also be a wise place, a place where one's thinking can reach beyond ordinary boundaries.

Emerson wrote, "Every thought is also a prison. . . . Therefore we love the poet, the inventor, who in any form, whether in an ode, or in an action, or in looks and behavior, has yielded us a new thought. He unlocks our chains and admits us to a new scene."

These inmates admitted me to a new scene. I'm no doubt freer as a result.

III

Whom Do You Need?

---

*Understanding human needs is
half the job of meeting them.*
—ADLAI STEVENSON

FRIENDS

"What is a friend?"

Christopher
Phillips

All forty or so of us Socrates Café regulars at Collage II Coffee-house feel drawn to this question tonight. It dawns on me that to one degree or another I think of most of the people here as friends. In fact, I cannot imagine engaging in Socratic inquiry without them. I need them. Yet I don't even know all of their last names, much less anything to speak of about their private lives except for the nuggets of information they offer here and there during our philosophical dialogues.

It also dawns on me that the question we've chosen to discuss this evening is the central question of Plato's dialogue *Lysis*, in which Socrates asks, In what way does one person become a friend of another? Even though this question is explored in some depth, Socrates says at the end of the dialogue that he and his cabal of chatterers failed to answer the question "What is a friend?" Perhaps tonight we'll have better fortune than he did.

"I think you first have to spell out what the potential qualities of a friend are," says Sharon Hayes. The first time Sharon came to Socrates Café, nine months ago, it was not on purpose. She and her musician husband Richard happened to be at Collage II nursing cups of coffee. She had just quit her job as a travel agent and they were trying to figure out what to do next. That particular night, she overheard us discussing "What is intuition?" She joined in. She'd quit her job on a hunch, and Socrates Café gave her an unexpected but welcome forum to better understand why she had taken the ostensibly crazy plunge of quitting—and to conclude that it was not so crazy after all. She's been a Socrates Café junkie ever since. "For me, mutual respect and empathy and the ability to forgive are the most important qualities," she then says.

90

"Why?" I ask her.

Sharon says, "Well, I'm not really comfortable articulating more about what a friend is other than what I've just said." She puts her arm around her husband. "Here's my best friend right here. He has all the qualities I've mentioned." Richard blushes.

"I enter each friendship with unconditional love," says Mike DeMatt. The youthful-looking, thoughtful man has been coming to Socrates Café for weeks now, and I still know hardly a thing about him, except that his insights tend to be uncommonly perceptive, and I can't imagine Socrates Café without his participation. "I have no expectations at all of my friends," he goes on to say.

"Is that really possible? " Ron asks him. Ron is a graduate student in sociology at the university. A warm and witty person with smiling hazel eyes and long blond hair, he has come to Socrates Café almost every week since day one. He has read widely and deeply, and he often is able to reveal hidden likenesses between wildly disparate subject areas. Ron and I have made the transition from being philosophical coconspirators, as is everyone else at Socrates Café, to becoming best friends. He is the only person here with whom I've shared my innermost hopes and dreams and fears, who has seen me at my worst and likes me none the worse for it. "Is it really possible to be friends unconditionally?" Ron then asks. "Is it possible to have no expectations?"

"I think so," Mike says to him. "I'm not saying that I expect my friends to have the same philosophy of friendship that I have."

"I've had a number of unilateral or one-sided friendships," says Jim Davis, his expression wry as ever. Jim has been coming to Socrates Café for months but I know next to nothing about him. He somehow manages to offer probing philosophical perspectives while revealing only the most general information about himself. "And I've also had some momentary friendships," he goes on to say.

Al Griffin, a retired insurance salesman, asks, "Can you be someone's friend if they aren't yours?" Al and I became friends soon after he happened into a Socrates Café gathering about six months earlier. Before that, Al, a tall, imposing man with a no-nonsense manner and a keen intelligence, had hardly read a word of philosophy. Now he seems to eat, sleep, and breathe it. He has returned to college and is well on his way to earning his bachelor's degree in philosophy. Al and I often while away the afternoon hours philosophizing together at a local diner. And wherever I facilitate a Socrates Café—at a senior center, at schools, at other cafés—Al often comes along. He and I are just about inseparable, and we must look like the odd couple when people see us together. He's just about always impeccably coiffed and garbed, while I tend to wear jeans and leather boots and a T-shirt, and prefer to shave as seldom as possible. Al and I aren't just friends; we're buddies. "I don't see how you can have a completely one-sided friendship," Al goes on to say to Jim.

"It happens all the time," Jim says. "You can choose to befriend someone with no expectation that they'll befriend you. Or even if you have that expectation, you can still be their friend even if they choose not to be yours."

"And what about momentary friendships?" Al asks. "Don't friendships have to stand the test of time? Isn't that one of the most important criteria of friendship?"

"I don't think so," Jim says. "I think you can have a one-minute friendship. If you do something nice for a person—treat someone as you would have them treat you—you are being their friend, you are engaging in a friendship. And even if a friendship is continuous, it is comprised of moments, and at any moment a friendship can be severed."

"It might be possible to look back on the origins of a friendship and discover that almost immediately two people had become 'fast friends,'" says Gale Pittman, her inquisitive eyes swimming behind prescription glasses with stylish frames. Since Gale first came to Socrates Café three months earlier and became hooked, she and I have run into each other everywhere—at the airport, at bookstores, at the local park. Each time, we've taken advantage of the unexpected encounter to get to know each other better. We both have decided that we are "meant" to become close friends. We still have a road to travel before we get there, though with each chance encounter we gradually reveal more and more about ourselves and like each other more and more. "But it takes a certain passage of time before it's possible for two friends to make such a discovery," she goes on to say.

"What exactly is it that they discover in order for them to realize that they have become friends?" I ask.

"Well, like Sharon said at the beginning of the discussion, they discover they have mutual respect and empathy for one another. And they discover that they enjoy one another's company."

"Do two people have to be alike in some fundamental way in order to be friends?"

"I think people can have extremely different personalities and still be best friends," Marta replies. "I'm pretty shy and softspoken, but my best friend is incredibly outgoing."

Looking at me, Hilda asks, "I think what you were trying to ask is whether a good person can only be friends with another good person, and whether an evil person can only be friends with another evil person."

"Among other things," I say. "But what you've just said makes me think of the section in Aristotle's *Nicomachean Ethics* where he said a 'perfect friendship' is one in which two people not only see one another as 'another self,' as reflections of one another, but who consider one another equally virtuous. Because of this, he believed that a good person couldn't be friends with a bad person."

"I don't think there is such a thing as a *completely* evil person," Marta says after much thought. "Besides that, I think that even the most wretched person probably has some good tendency, even if it's well hidden. For instance, I've read about how even the most despicable person often has a pet that he loves deeply and dotes on. This pet, I think, is his friend, probably his best and only friend. And I think even the most virtuous person has probably gone astray at one time or another in his life. For me, this awareness of how easy it is to stray from the 'straight and narrow' makes me feel a kinship to the so-called bad person."

"I agree," says Hilda. She always comes alone to Socrates Café, and on the numerous occasions I've seen her about town, she's never been accompanied by anyone else. "And I've read about people who are evil in many respects and yet are fiercely loyal to their friends. For instance, I've read that many of the Nazis who committed such heinous atrocities at concentration camps somehow were also true-blue friends to a select few, and would put their lives on the line for these friends."

"Okay," I say, "but this still seems at least to suggest that people are friends with people of similar moral character. The people you just described as friends shared the same abhorrent character in terms of their treatment of concentration camp victims. And for all I know, in some sick way, they may have thought of themselves as good people. So I'm wondering if it's almost always the case that only people of similar moral scruples, or lack thereof—people who have similar conceptions of right and wrong, of good and evil—can be friends with one another."

"I'm not sure if it's always the case, but I think it's often the case," says Winston, a man of impossible-to-guess age who attends every Socrates Café. He sits in a remote corner, his crossed leg moving vigorously as he pretends to be—or perhaps is—absorbed in whatever book he happens to have open on that particular evening. "But I think there are always exceptions," he goes on to say. "I just read this mystery by Walter Mosley called *A Red Death*. And the main character, Easy Rawlins, speaks of his best friend Raymond as 'the truest friend' he ever had. But he also says of Raymond, 'If there is such a thing as true evil, he is that too.' His friend Raymond will kill anyone he thinks has wronged him without losing a minute's sleep over it. But he can also be a true-blue friend, and several times he's gotten Easy Rollins out of the worst kinds of jams."

He closes his book. "I think what I'm trying to get at is that it's dicey at best to try to oversimplify this. I think we've got to look at the fact that most people have extreme contradictions within them. They probably have seeds of both good and evil, even if it is the case that they are disciplined or 'good' enough to never feel compelled to act upon their evil impulses."

"I don't agree with you," says a woman named Kathie who came to Socrates Café for the first time last week. "I think some people are almost completely good and some are almost completely evil, and this affects the way friendships are formed. For years my brother has been an English teacher for inmates at a maximum security prison. He's become friends with a number of them. Some are rapists, some are murderers. But he's still their friend. Because over the course of time he's been able to find the good in them. And I think because he's befriended them, they've become better people."

"I think he's tapped into the goodness in them," Frank Lauterberg responds. "But if that's so, then he's friends with 'the good part' of their nature. Because as you've said, this is the side in them that he's helped to bring out. So I'm not sure if we can really say that this is an instance of a good person being friends with bad people."

Frank pauses before adding, "We'll probably have to wait till another Socrates Café to delve into this in detail, but it's just occurred to me that we've been speaking of good and evil people, instead of good and evil acts that people commit. I don't think people are innately good or evil, only that they do good, or evil."

"I agree," another participant says. "Besides that, can't one person's good be another person's evil?"

Christopher
Phillips

The Socrates of Plato's *Republic* believed that the difference between good and evil is not a mere matter of opinion. He believed that rigorous inquiry into the nature of good and evil would lead to knowledge that would enable a person clearly to tell the difference between the two. "Let each one of us . . . seek and follow one thing only, to learn and discern between good and evil," he said. But Michel de Montaigne begins an essay with the declaration that "the taste of good and evil depends in large part on the opinion we have of them." Baruch Spinoza wrote that the concepts of good and evil "indicate nothing positive in things considered in themselves, nor are they anything else than modes of thought. . . . One and the same thing may at the same time be both good and evil, or indifferent." He believed it all depended on whether a person judged the thing, or act, to be evil.

Some animal welfare activists consider it a heinous and even evil act to slaughter an animal, much less to eat meat, and some consider people who commit such acts to be evil. There are other animal welfare activists who don't consider it evil to slaughter an animal, unless it is done in what they consider an inhumane way. Still others consider it good in virtually every way to slaughter an animal for food—depending on the animal. For some, it would be perfectly all right to slaughter a cow, but not a horse, which they consider a noble beast. For others, it would be evil to slaughter a cow, for religious reasons. Yet for others, it is okay and even customary to eat a cat or a dog. But unlike Spinoza, I don't think these examples indicate that whether an act is evil or not simply boils down to "the opinion we have" of it, that it's all relative or all a matter of "cultural norms." My own reading across the disciplines on the subject of evil, and the Socrates Café dialogues I've held that touch on this subject, lead me to conclude that most of us hold remarkably similar views on what criteria should be used to judge whether an act is evil—namely, that such an act is morally bad or wrong, that it is usually intentional, and that it either threatens or brings harm to someone or something. Where we often disagree sharply is on which specific acts are evil ones. Our widely varying belief systems color which acts we believe to be morally bad or wrong, or intentionally harmful. So the specific contexts in which each of us believes evil to have occurred often differ dramatically.

Frank eventually says, "I agree that no one is completely good or evil. During my college years, I was a literacy volunteer for teens in a juvenile detention program. Some of them had committed awful crimes. But the one thing I realized, after spending a great deal of time with them, was how similar I was, in many ways, to them. I think of what Nietzsche said, 'I looked into the abyss and saw myself.' I could see myself in these people. I could see that I had the potential to commit the types of crimes they committed." He smiles and says, "Which leads me to another quote: 'There but for the grace of God go I.' It was humbling to realize how similar I am in nature to these teens I was working with. It made me much more empathetic, and I can say that several of them became my friends and confidants every bit as much as I became theirs."

"I want to comment on this notion of a friend being a confidant," says eighteen-year-old Jasmine, who graduates from high school in a few short months and is, as she put it when we talked before Socrates Café got under way, "excited out of her mind" that she was accepted at Princeton University, where she plans to

Christopher
Phillips

major in philosophy. "Several years ago, my best friend in the whole world confided to me that her stepfather had been sexually abusing her since she was six. Before she told me this, she made me promise not to tell anyone what she was about to share with me. And I did promise her I wouldn't. For weeks I kept it to myself. But every time I thought of how she was suffering, I felt I was betraying her by not trying to do something that might help her. Finally I told our history teacher, who'd befriended me once when I had a problem. I was just hoping she'd give me some advice about what to do, but she said that as a teacher, it was her responsibility to report cases of suspected abuse as soon as they were reported to her. She immediately reported what I told her to social services, and someone from social services intervened very quickly. My best friend's stepdad was taken into custody not long afterward. My teacher kept telling me I 'did the right thing' in coming forward and telling her. But my best friend didn't think so. She told me I'd betrayed her and that I was now her worst enemy. She transferred to another school, and we didn't speak to each other again—until last month. She called me to thank me for what I did way back when. She said that I saved her life. She said she'd been on the verge of committing suicide before I told our history teacher. Even though for a long while she felt even worse after her stepdad was arrested, she told me that after months of counseling, she began to realize that nothing that had happened was her fault in any way, and that her stepdad was the one who had betrayed her, not me. And she told me that only a best friend would have risked our friendship to do what I did for her."

She pauses and draws a deep breath. A couple of people are quietly crying. "So, for me," Jasmine says, "a friend is someone who always has your best interests at heart. A friend may not always seem to do the right thing, and some things she does on your behalf may not work out exactly as intended . . . but her heart is always in the right place."

No one says a word for a long while. What if you act with the best of intentions but the outcome of your action doesn't turn out as intended? Does this mean that at least to some extent your actions are determined by forces beyond your control? Or is there no such thing as chance or fate, and even if you don't know it, is some "higher power" pulling the cosmic strings and ensuring that everything happens for the best? Epictetus, a Stoic moral philosopher in the first and second century A.D. who established a school of philosophy after being freed as a slave, believed that while we can't control all the elements, we are autonomous in the sense that we can control how we react to the vicissitudes of existence. "We must make the best of those things that are in our power, and take the rest as nature gives it," he wrote. In a similar vein, Friedrich Nietzsche asserted that while we are not complete masters of our fate, we're not passive victims either. Rather, he said, we're cocreators of our destiny. Just as there are external forces that play a part in determining the course of our actions, Nietzsche believed that we too are an indispensable force to be reckoned with, and that we can carve out a unique existence even if, for better or worse, it does not turn out precisely as planned.

"What else can we say about friendship?" I ask the group after a powerful silence.

"I think one of the central features of friendship is that friends have to strive for a quid pro quo," says Sara, who as always is wide-eyed and attentive to every word said. She has attended Socrates Café for months but I know nothing about her except that we share a passion for philosophizing.

"I don't buy into the notion of a quid pro quo as a ground for friendship," Al Griffin says in his typical blunt way. "Friendships don't have to be based on some measure of equality."

"I think maybe you should consider looking at quid pro quo in a different way," I say to Al. "For instance, if one friend performs one favor and the other friend performs a thousand, there's still favors that have been carried out by both. That one favor may have been a huge one that made a tremendous impact on the friend's life, while the thousand favors the other friend did may have been relatively inconsequential. So maybe there is an equality, a balance, but not in the way you're thinking about it."

Christopher
Phillips

"Maybe," Al says, biting his lower lip, a habit I 'd long since come to know meant he was thinking hard. "Maybe."

"I have a friend who lives in Hawaii whom I write or call all the time," says a woman wearing a U2 T-shirt who is a newcomer to Socrates Café. "But she rarely takes the initiative to stay in touch. So I've been thinking about whether I should quit staying in touch with her. I'm tired of always having to initiate our correspondence. I resent it."

"But why can't both friends recognize that they are meeting each other's needs, even if the tally of who contacts whom is way out of balance?" I ask her. "I have one friend who rarely writes to me or anyone else. So when I get a letter from her, it's really a special occasion. I scribble letters to her all the time, but hers are a thousand times more thoughtful than mine. So in my case, I wonder if the balance is out of whack, but in her favor, not mine."

After a comfortable silence, Tim Raymond says, "I think friendship is something that entails survival." Several years earlier, Tim suffered a workplace accident that left him disabled. The one time Tim spoke of what happened, he seemed neither resigned nor depressed, neither overly upbeat nor Pollyannaish. He approaches life with a gentle and thoughtful disposition and he appears to savor every moment like few people I've ever met. "The more and more time that passes and people still remain friends, the stronger their friendship," he says. "As time passes, mistakes are made, feelings are hurt. Yet friendship endures. So survival, or endurance, is a criterion."

Twelve-year-old Jeffrey Ingram abruptly stops thumbing through the magazine he has brought with him. His blue eyes peering beneath dark bangs, he says with a sort of friendly smirk, "All of you are speaking about friendship in terms of two people. But what about friendships in severals or in bunches?" Jeffrey is a student at one of the elementary schools where I regularly philosophize with children. When I first visited his class and introduced myself as a philosopher, Jeffrey looked at me as if I were an alien. He'd never heard of a philosopher before. The more I told Jeffrey and his classmates about what I do, the more he wanted to know. I don't think I've ever met such a good listener, and I've certainly never met someone so young who has taken such a genuine interest in philosophy. Engaging in philosophical inquiry at his school in the daytime isn't sufficient for Jeffrey, so his mom takes him to Socrates Café each Tuesday night. An hour might pass and Jeffrey might not say a word. But when he finally chooses to make an observation, he comes up with an insight the rest of us have overlooked.

"He's absolutely right," says Laurie Sellers. "In fact, most of my friendships are in bunches. I have groups of friends."

"Or," I say, "can't we speak of friendship in terms of just one person? Can't I be my own friend?"

"I think so," says a Socrates Café newcomer. "But I think whether you're talking about being friends with yourself, or with another, or with many others, it seems that to a certain degree you have to be nonjudgmental if you're going to stay friends over the long haul."

"Is this really true?" I ask. "Or is it the case that a friend can be highly judgmental, but not in a bad way? Who best to judge someone and offer constructive criticism than one's best friend?"

"I agree with you," Ron says. "Nietzsche said that friends should be educators to one another. And if they were going to be educators in the way he meant it, they not only could not be sentimental, but to a degree they had to be judgmental. To him it was a friend's responsibility to help a friend gain self-mastery."

We again fall silent for a spell as we reflect on all the notions of friendship we've considered. "What are friends for?" Richard Hayes asks after a while.

"What do you mean?" another participant asks.

"Well, the folks in the dialogue in Plato's *Lysis* came to a pretty quick agreement that friends are of use to one another in some way, otherwise they wouldn't be friends. I'm wondering what all of you think about that."

"I think it's true, without a doubt," says Sharon. "I bet even those who say they expect nothing of their friends feel their friends are of use to them, even if they've never articulated what that use is. Their friends fill some need. I'm not saying they're exploited or 'used,' but I am saying that they are in some sense useful."

"What kind of needs might they fill?" I ask.

"Well, in my case, I can say that everyone, from my best friend to my most fair-weather friend, makes me feel less alone in the world," she replies. "For me, they're all filling one of my most basic needs. I believe Kant said something to the effect that in friendship, everything is an end instead of only a means. I think he meant that friends strive to please one another. They may satisfy themselves in the process, but what they do is ultimately for the sake of the other. For instance, I might invite you to go camping with me. And one of the reasons I might do this is because I don't like to camp alone. But my higher motive is to bring you along on a trip that I feel sure you'd enjoy tremendously, especially because I know how much you like to camp."

There seems no end to questions: What is a good friendship? What constitutes a failed friendship? Is there such a thing as a destructive friendship? How are friendships formed? How are friendships different from other types of relationships? How are friendships formed and how are they broken? Can a book be your friend? The dialogue goes on far longer than usual. It is approaching midnight. We seem reluctant to bring the dialogue to a close, but finally I ask for a few final reflections.

Ann is one of the very last to speak. Her blond hair peaks out through a brightly wrapped hat. Ann calls me "the professor." I tell her I'm not a professor, that I am the furthest thing from a professor. But to Ann, I am "the professor," and that's that. The very first time Ann attended Socrates Café months ago, she revealed enough bits and pieces about her life to make it clear that she has overcome daunting trials and tribulations. This effervescent woman emerged from the experience as a survivor who uses her past not as a reason to brood or to regret time wasted, but as a springboard for her singularly empathetic and independent way of thinking. I know that she has come to see Socrates Café as a haven of sorts. And today, as usual, she has been listening intently to everyone's comments. And as usual, she says nothing herself until almost the very end.

"The poet and playwright Goethe said that friends 'enhance each other,'" Ann now says. "I agree with him—almost. To me, a friend is someone who accepts you when you're at your very worst, but inspires you to be a better person."

"Amen," Sharon says.

Then I say, "I think this community here is my friend. The dialogue binds us together."

There is another pleasant silence. I think of the friends I have let down, or who have let me down, in ways both great and small over the years. I think of friends who have weathered many highs and lows with me. And I think of how many of these friendships not only have survived but have somehow thrived in spite of, or because of, our willingness to accept one another at our worst—because this willingness has been an impetus for us to become better and better friends and human beings.

"Well, my friends," I say at last, "it's something to keep thinking about."

I look at Al, at Richard, at Ann, at Tim, at Sharon, at Gale, and finally at Ron. I want to say something else. I'm moving to the Bay Area of California the next day. I have no doubts that I'm leaving the Socrates Café here in good hands; there are now a number of others who adeptly facilitate the dialogues and who will carry the torch. But while I'm looking forward to helping start a number of Socrates Cafés at various venues in California soon after I arrive, the decision to move has been a wrenching one. I wonder if I'll ever make friends there who will become as dear to me as these people here. I want somehow to let everyone here know how much they mean to me. But I cannot find the words.

Sharon finds them for me. "We love you too," she says.

AND THE CHILDREN SHALL LEAD ME

I need children to philosophize with.

No one questions, no one wonders, no one examines, like children. It is not simply that children love questions but that they *live* questions.

The first time I visited a group of fifth-grade students at a school not far from Seattle, Washington, I started out by saying, "Philosophy begins with a sense of wonder," which is straight from Aristotle's *Nicomachean Ethics* and very similar to what Socrates says in Plato's *Theaetetus*, namely that a sense of wonder is "the mark of the philosopher."

"What is wonder?" one of the children immediately queried, before I had a chance to continue. I'd given the same "sense of wonder" spiel to numerous groups of adults, but this was the first time anyone had ever asked me this question.

"What do you take wonder to mean?" I asked in turn.

"I'm not sure," he replied. He brushed away his dark brown bangs and looked squarely at me, his face animated, and then said, "I can tell you what I wonder *about*, but I'm not sure if that's the same thing as what wonder *means*."

"It sounds like a great way to find out more about what wonder means," I said.

"I wonder what other kids think of me," he said softly. "I wonder what they see. I wonder if they see a good person." He seemed to be finished, but then he said, "Sometimes I'm kind of jealous of the other kids because they can see my face, and I'll never be able to, except in a mirror—and mirrors always distort."

His teacher was clearly amazed by this revelation. She told me later that he rarely said a word in class, and had never before revealed anything about himself. I wanted to tell her, "But this is philosophy. Philosophy works wonders with kids, and kids work wonders with philosophy."

In Charles Dickens' *Hard Times*, the notorious Thomas Gradgrind, lover of cold hard facts and nothing but facts, exhorts his daughter, "Never wonder!" because he believed the ability to reason should be cultivated "without stooping to the cultivation of the sentiments and affections." Socrates, on the other hand, believed that one's reasoning powers could not be nurtured and honed *without* wondering.

Children wonder ceaselessly. In *The Making of the Modern Mind,* John Herman Randall, Jr., noted that individuals "whose infancy is prolonged" are "able to continue learning when others have reached the limits of their powers and natural resources." In my case, there is little question that my "infancy" has been "prolonged"—that my questioning nature and love of learning has been continually cultivated—in large measure because I philosophize regularly with children.

Christopher Phillips

Children, more than any others with whom I engage in philosophical inquiry, inform me. They help me see. Moreover, it has been my experience that most children do not know how *not* to be honest. Their questioning, and their attempt to come up with answers, has an integrity that is lacking with many adults. And children possess an exemplary readiness and willingness to "self-correct" their philosophy whenever it becomes clear that the point of view they had been advocating does not pass muster after all.

Jean Piaget, a biologist-turned-psychologist who, starting in the 1920s, made it his life's work to observe and explain the development of the child's mind, argued that the thought of children resembled that of pre-Socratic thinkers, in that neither had a cohesive system of beliefs. Earlier, the American pragmatist philosopher William James had written about the "blooming buzzing confusion" of a youngster's world. But Jerome Bruner, a New York University professor of psychology noted for his groundbreaking work in the emerging field of cultural psychology, holds that such a view belies a wealth of compelling evidence. In his extensive research on the mental development of children and on their experiential relationships with their cultural milieu, Bruner has found that even infants and preschoolers are inquisitive seekers "acting not directly *on* 'the world'" but rather "on beliefs" they hold "*about* the world." Very early on in the developmental process, he asserts, children are already striving to make sense of the world and their culture. They are "much smarter, more cognitively proactive rather than reactive, . . . than had been previously suspected," and far from seeing the world as a blooming buzzing confusion, they are highly "attentive to the immediate social world around them" and have formulated belief systems far more sophisticated than those they'd previously been given credit for.

In his classic *How Children Learn,* John Holt, one of this country's leading educational and social critics, who spent his professional life studying how children think and learn, asserted that "young children tend to learn better than grownups" because they "have a style of learning that fits their condition, and which they use naturally and well until we train them out of it." Holt lamented that adults all too often replace children's innate and insatiable curiosity—which he said is the source for "a natural and powerful way of thinking"—with dessicated and rigid learning techniques that are doomed to destroy their love of learning. "Gears, twigs, leaves, little children love the world," wrote Holt. "That is why they are so good at learning about it. For it is love, not tricks and techniques of thought, that lies at the heart of all true learning. Can we bring ourselves to let children learn and grow through that love?"

BEYOND BELIEF

Our philosophizing for the day has just come to an end. All the children have already left for recess. All except Jeremy, who lingers in the Bay Area elementary school library, where our weekly philosophy discussion is held. He is wringing his hands, which he seems to be studying with immense concentration.

"What did you think of the discussion?" I ask him.

In our dialogue today, we made a valiant attempt to answer the question "What is belief?" During the discussion, Jeremy related how he and his brother often look out their bedroom window at night when the rest of his family is asleep. "Sometimes we see lights that don't seem to be attached to anything flying through the sky," he'd said at one point. "My little brother says they're UFOs. I tell him they're just airplanes. But he won't believe me."

Christopher Phillips

"But you won't believe him either," I said to him.

To which he replied, "That's because I know what he said isn't true."

I pressed him, "But don't you think he believed it was true?"

Jeremy nodded. I wanted him and the other kids to consider the time-honored philosophical conundrum whether beliefs are no more or less than those things which we take to be true, regardless of how we arrived at them. I was specifically thinking about Plato's *Theaetetus*, in which Socrates explores ways in which a belief can be said to be articulate: the premise at the outset was that if a belief can be expressed in words, it is articulate. But Socrates delved further and concluded that only if you can offer a convincing analysis of why you believe what you do—in this case, why Jeremy believed the object he saw was an airplane—can that belief be considered articulate.

Scott, one of the other kids, then asked Jeremy how he could be so sure what he and his brother saw were planes and not UFOs. Jeremy replied, "Because I've seen the same lights in the sky at dusk when there's still some daylight. And the lights are always attached to airplanes. So I concluded that if that's what they always are at dusk, then that must be what they are at night when all you can see are the lights and not the planes." Jeremy has applied a form of the scientific method of thinking, based on experience and observation and deductive reasoning, to come to this compelling conclusion.

But Scott, for one, was not completely swayed. "But how can you *prove* that it's not a UFO?" he asked Jeremy.

"I guess I can't," Jeremy replied. "But I think I have more evidence that it's an airplane than my brother does that it's a UFO. And I bet someday that my brother'll realize it's not a UFO. Just like he used to believe in Santa Claus and now he knows Santa Claus isn't really real."

This inspired me to ask Jeremy, "How did he come to believe Santa Claus wasn't real?"

Jeremy thought about this for a while and then shrugged. "I guess the same way I did. No evidence. Santa Claus became, for me, I guess, kind of a fairy tale."

"So what does that say about beliefs?" I asked him.

Again the thoughtful child took his time in mulling this over before replying, "A belief is something I think I know is true or false. But if it's false—like if it's false that the lights in the sky are from a UFO—then it's a *mistaken* belief."

Jeremy's thoughtful reply brought to mind one of my favorite philosophers, the largely unsung nineteenth-century British philosopher William Kingdon Clifford. In his little-known essay "Origins of Belief," Clifford discusses belief in terms of whether a person's action can be said to be right or wrong. "The question of right or wrong has to do with the origin of his belief," wrote Clifford, "not the matter of it; not what it was, but how he got it; not whether it turned out to be true or false, but whether he had a right to believe on such evidence as was before him." Clifford believed that "sincere convictions," unless honestly earned by means of the type of patient inquiry Jeremy employed, are "stolen by listening to the voice of prejudice and passion."

Christopher Phillips

His contemporary, the American philosopher and Harvard professor William James, developed a different sort of philosophy in his particular variety of pragmatism. In his popular essay "Will to Believe," James claimed that there are situations in which "abandoning such rigorous procedures" of inquiry as those advocated by Clifford "is justified." The 'right to believe' without sufficient evidence is allowable if it works," maintained James. To James, if a belief seems compelling and of great consequence, then we owe it to ourselves to ask: "Am I to accept it or go without it?" James' choice is: Accept it. "Our errors are surely not such awfully solemn things," he writes. "In a world where we are so certain to incur them in spite of all our caution, a certain lightness of heart seems healthier than this excessive nervousness on their behalf." Jeremy, who came to his sincere conviction (or lack thereof) about Santa Claus by means of patient inquiry, evidently sides with Clifford over James in their conflicting philosophies about belief.

Jeremy lives in a two-room apartment with his parents and seven siblings. His three older brothers have already dropped out of school. I often tell the unusually bright and perceptive child, and exceptional student, that I hope he'll go to college. But whenever I used to say this, he typically gave me an expression that seems to indicate he thinks this is beyond his reach, something he shouldn't dare to believe might be a possibility lest his belief be dashed. But then I took him to tour a local college. We visited several classes, picked up a catalogue and looked through it together, and I explained to him about the scholarships available, and showed him the admissions and scholarship application forms. He was so excited after our trip that now he talks often, and knowledgeably, about college. It no longer seems such an intimidating and beyond-his-grasp place. Slowly but surely, he is developing a sincere self-belief that he can and will one day go to college. Jeremy clearly is pleased that I've taken such an interest in him, and I in turn get a great deal of satisfaction out of seeing this special child flourish and develop self-confidence.

But today, at the end of our weekly gathering, Jeremy is unusually reticent after I ask him how he liked this particular philosophical discussion. He does not respond to my question for a long time. He rocks back and forth on the heels of his feet. He makes a halfhearted attempt to brush his long bangs away from his eyes. Finally he takes a deep breath and says to me in a barely audible whisper, "My dad tried to make me believe that he didn't punch me last night and make my tooth bleed." His voice becomes firmer as he says, "But he did. I know he did." He goes on to tell me that when he went to tell his mom, his dad denied everything. He tells me that his dad sounded so convincing that he almost believed him himself. "He lies," Jeremy then says. He shows me his newly grown-in front tooth. It is loose and rimed with dried blood. The demeanor of this innately good-natured child betrays a mixture of anger and hurt and confusion. He will never again be as innocent as a child his age deserves to be. "I know what to believe and what not to believe," the fifth grader then says, speaking as much to himself as to me.

There is no doubt in my mind that Jeremy's father has abused him, and I report to his teacher what he has just told me. As I relate this to the teacher, who assures me she'll contact the city's social services department at once, it dawns on me that almost certainly Jeremy wouldn't have revealed to me that his father had abused him if we hadn't happened to discuss "What is belief?" that day.

Christopher Phillips

YOUNG SOPHISTICATES

Just as children can make astute distinctions between honesty and dishonesty, between truth and lies, they know the difference between trying their level best, between devoting their heart and soul and mind, their imaginative and critical capacities, to answering a question philosophically and making a halfhearted attempt to come up with "any old answer," legitimate or otherwise, that comes to mind. "Okay, fair enough," an adult might respond. "Maybe. But they're not being honest so much as they are speaking as those do who have yet to develop sophisticated perspectives." Oh, but they do have sophisticated perspectives, and a Socratic dialogue with children gives them the opportunity to show just how sophisticated their views can be.

THE PHILOSOPHERS CLUB

"What is silence?"

It is Wednesday and our twice-weekly gang meeting begins at 2 P.M. sharp. I am with twenty-one fourth and fifth graders at Cesar Chavez Elementary School, a brightly painted school in the heart of San Francisco's vibrant but impoverished Mission District. The children and I are in the school library seated on comfortable sofas. We like meeting in the library. It has an informal, relaxed atmosphere. And it's easy for me to sneak in cookies and juice. In many ways, this place is an oasis for the kids from the outside world, where drug dealers abound and young toughs who belong to gangs with names like the Reds and the Blues and the North Street Gang haunt nearby street corners.

Our gang is called the Philosophers Club. When, several years ago, I first visited with these children, who live in an area with a school dropout rate that is woefully high, they'd never before heard of the word philosophy. Now they can't imagine life without it. "We philosophers think up questions so we can think up answers, so we can think up more questions" is how my philosopher friend Rafi, now nine, a fourth grader at Cesar Chavez, describes the philosophical pursuit.

It was soft-spoken Wilson, a kid from Ecuador with penetrating almond-shaped blue eyes, who proposed early on that we call ourselves the Philosophers Club. His fellow young philosophers loved the name. It stuck.

And now, at this latest club meeting, he has asked us, "What is silence?"

His question immediately brings to mind a number of perspectives on silence. I had recently reread the Brazilian educator Paolo Freire's *Pedagogy of the Oppressed*, in which he writes of a "culture of silence" composed of people who, because of a lifetime of deprivation and oppression, fatalistically accept that they have little or no control over their lives. I think of the parents of these children, many of whom are in such straits. Maurice Merleau-Ponty, a French phenomenologist, offers a much different perspective on silence. *In The Visible and the Invisible*, he describes silence as the ground for all language: "My silence in both speaking and listening is necessary for my role as an active participant in my dialogue with the world." But some forms of silence can indicate that one is shirking a critical opportunity to engage in dialogue. In her acclaimed *The Language of Silence: West German Literature and the Holocaust,* Ernestine Schlant, a professor of comparative literature, analyzes West German literature—

specifically, noted novels by non-Jewish German authors—and its attempts to come to terms with the Holocaust and its impact on postwar West German society. She comes to the disturbing conclusion that in such literature there all too often is a "language of silence" in which the victims and their suffering are overlooked.

My silent reflections are cut off when Wilson amends his initial question by saying, "Well, actually, what I really want to know is, is it possible to be silent if everyone else around you is screaming?"

He can see that I am slow on the uptake, so he explains, "Even when I try to go to sleep at night, I hear screaming. I hear gangs outside screaming. I hear the neighbors screaming. So I can't be silent even if I'm silent."

He pauses. We silently wait for him to complete his thought. Then he says, "So I guess what I'm really wondering is, if everyone around you is screaming, can you really be silent? Because you can still hear everybody else even if you plug up your ears."

"Let's experiment," I say. We take turns stopping up our ears while everyone else in the Philosophers Club screams. Sure enough, the screaming foils our best attempts to create a wall of silence around us. So, we collectively conclude, it is in fact impossible to "be" silent, to be in a state of silence, with everyone screaming around you.

But then Juan Carlos, who is from Peru and is the other unusually silent kid in our group, says, "Even if it's possible for someone to block out all the noise around him, it's still impossible for him to be silent."

He can see by my expression that I don't quite understand what he's getting at. But like all the Philosophers Club kids, he's patient with me, because he knows adults like me sometime have trouble philosophizing with the same keenness as children. So he explains to me, "You can't be silent to yourself, even if you are silent to everyone else. I may not talk out loud, but I still talk to myself. I still have conversations with myself inside my head, even if no one else can hear me. I can't turn off the voices in my head. So that's not being silent. Is it?"

We again experiment. We all try to be completely silent to ourselves, to "turn off" the voice or voices in our minds. Each of us finds it an impossible feat.

We fall outwardly silent, concentrating on our voices within. What seem like minutes pass. "You can be silent but not completely silent," Rafi, a special-education student from Guatemala, says finally, breaking the silence.

"How so?" I ask.

"Well, we've been silent, on the outside, but not inside our heads," he says. "So we have been silent. Just not completely silent."

Rafi's teacher's aide happens to be sitting in on this particular discussion and now has a look of astonishment on his face. Just after the gathering comes to an end, the instructor takes me aside and says to me, "I didn't think Rafi was capable of thinking things like that." He adds a bit sheepishly, "I'm not capable of thinking like that."

Indeed, Rafi may have learning deficiencies, but there seem to be few limitations on his ability to transcend them. In fact, despite his learning deficiencies, Rafi and the rest of the members of the Philosophers Club are gifted learners in my estimation.

Which prompts me to ask: What is gifted?

Whenever I first philosophize with a group of kids, I bring a glass half filled with water. And I ask the kids, "Is the glass half empty or half full?" The last time I did this with a group of kids singled out as "gifted," they argued among themselves that the glass has to be one or the other, either empty or full. They never considered other possibilities.

Not so the members of the Philosophers Club. "It's half empty *and* half full," Carmen said when I posed the question to them. "It's half full of water and half empty of water."

Then Estefania said, "It's half empty and half empty! It's half empty of air and half empty of water." The doe-eyed fifth grader smiles widely, pleased with herself at this insight.

This prompted fair-haired, fair-skinned Arturo, who is from Mexico, to say, "It's completely full. It's full of water and air molecules."

To which Pilar, a cherubic-faced child who also hails from Mexico, chimed in, "But it's completely empty too, empty of lots of things. It's empty of everything but water and air."

Then Rafi, who as usual waited a long time before saying a word, said, "What about that thing in the middle there?

I looked at the glass and I looked at him. I didn't see what he saw. "What do you mean?"

He took the glass from me and jiggled it so the surface of the water moved. "There," he said. "Where the water and the air meet. That doesn't have anything to do with empty or full, does it?"

Here is a kid who would be perfectly at home, more than holding his own, hunched over with the ancient Greek philosopher Zeno of Elea, discussing his famous paradoxes. In one of his paradoxes, Zeno says that in order to travel from point A to point B, you first have to cross half that distance. But in order to make it to that halfway point, he notes that first you have to cover half that distance . . . but first you have to cover half that distance, and half of that distance, and so on, ad infinitum. In fact, in order to even get started on the journey, you have to cross an infinite number of points—a feat that Zeno says can't be accomplished in any finite time period. So, he concludes, it has to be impossible even to take the first step. And so I wonder what Zeno would have to say to Rafi about how, or whether, the divide between the air and water in the glass can ever be bridged, or if there is an infinite separation between the two in finite space—a seeming paradox every bit as perplexing as the one Zeno offered on traversing the distance between points A and B.

All these kids have seen things in this glass that no other group of kids with whom I've philosophized has ever seen. They have opened my eyes.

So again, I ask: Who is gifted? What does it mean to be gifted? In relation to seeking Socrates, I can tell you, hands down, that the most gifted kids I've ever encountered are those in the Philosophers Club at Cesar Chavez Elementary School. While in some cases their abilities in the three Rs may be below par, their ability in "the fourth R"—the ability to reason—is without equal.

As I write this, I see Rafi bursting out of his chair, unable to contain his excitement over his latest philosophical finding. I see his hands kneading his furrowed brow, massaging his mind, as he thinks. I see him leaning forward over the table, smiling, revealing deep dimples, his hands clenching and unclenching as he immerses himself in the dialogue. I see him thinking about speaking but choosing not to, not just yet, as he continues to formulate the words and thoughts and concepts that are spilling over one another in his mind, jostling and jousting for position. I see the look of peace envelop him as he puts them in place and then slowly thinks his thoughts out loud.

Each of these kids reminds me of Socrates. Especially Rafi. He has the heart and soul and mind—and unquenchable curiosity—of a philosopher and a poet and a scientist all rolled into one.

Christopher
Phillips

YOUNGER FOLKS AND OLDER FOLKS

Children and seniors—or, as I call them, younger folks and older folks—are kindred spirits. But many of the things they hold in common put into stark relief the shortcomings in the rest of us, and in our society. Older folks all too often are shunted off to nursing homes and senior residence complexes, many of which are quite fancy and handsome and provide nonstop programs of rather mindless activities. But none of this compensates for the loss of independence, of home, of family, of identity. Older folks are unusually reflective. But few want to reflect with them. Older folks are prone to tell it like it is. But few want to hear it like it is. The older they are, the more innocent, the more vulnerable, the more thoughtful—the more childlike—they become. And as they become more like children, those adults who are not yet stigmatized with the label of "senior citizen" treat their older counterparts in the same way they tend to treat children—condescendingly, at times demeaningly, at times even abusively.

Like older folks, children are honest to a fault. What's more, "regular adults" often treat children, just like they treat older folks, as if they are to be seen and not heard. Who has time to listen? Parents are too busy making ends meet or moving full speed ahead in their careers. Many children know their "primary" caregivers—day care sitters, nannies, what have you—better than their own parents.

The lamentable result is that all too often children and seniors are at the margins of society, castoffs. But their peculiar status in society also unites them: younger folks and older folks *need* each other. They need each other to philosophize with. Unlike so many adults, older folks share with children a tenacious and passionate desire to keep asking and asking and asking: *Why? Why? Why?*

SO OLD?

It is early spring and a group of thirty-six seniors and children are gathered around a long rectangular table in a well-lit and spacious seminar room in Montclair, New Jersey. At 2 P.M. sharp, third-grade teacher Brenda Saunders arrives with her students in tow. They have walked over from their elementary school, about a hundred yards away. All of the seniors—regular participants at various Socrates Cafés I'd helped establish at local coffeehouses and senior residences—have already arrived.

In all, there are eighteen younger folks and eighteen older folks. And there is me, somewhere in the middle, but most definitely edging closer in age to the older folks. In an unabashed act of social engineering, I have arranged the seating so the children and seniors sit in alternate seats. I know that none of the younger folks have met any of the older folks who will be taking part. Yet from the moment they plunk themselves down in their seats, the younger folks and older folks begin talking to one another—between gulps of lemonade and bites of chocolate chip cookies—as if they were long-lost friends.

When I began inviting older Socrates Café participants from throughout the area to take part in this dialogue, to a person they told me they wouldn't miss it for the world. One told me, "You're giving me a chance to learn from our youngest teachers."

When I ask for a question to discuss, Helen, one of the older folks taking part, looks perplexed. First she puts her hand up, but then she puts it down. Then she puts it up again. "I have a question," she says.

"Okay," I say.

"The other day I told someone I was taking college classes, and then, when I told her how old I am, she said, 'You're not so old,'" Helen relates. "At the time, what she said didn't bother me. But now I wonder what she meant. I wonder if she even knew what she was talking about. I mean, I'm wondering . . . how old is 'so old'?"

"Who can answer that?" I ask.

Tia's hand shoots up immediately, even though her mouth is half filled with a cookie. "So old,'" the thoughtful third grader says, "is, like, when you're around a hundred."

"Why do say that?" I ask.

"Because when you're ninety you're old, and when you're a hundred you're *so* old."

"So it seems you're equating 'so old' with 'really old,'" I say. "So . . . why is it that a hundred is 'so old' and ninety isn't?"

"A hundred just sounds right," she says, affecting a seraphic grin.

"It just sounds right," I repeat. "Hmmmm . . . Let's see if we can get some others to help us."

Her classmate Alex can hardly contain himself, so anxious is he to pitch in right away. "If you're young, even ten is very old or 'so old' to you. If you're forty, then sixty is old to you," says Alex, who is by far the tallest student in his class and looks to be at least two years older than he is. "So whether something is 'so old' depends on how old you are. If you're ten and you know someone who is sixty, then they are 'so old.'"

"But what is old? How can you say what 'so old' is—in the way you're equating the term, or in any other way we might look at it—unless we know what old itself is?"

He mulls this over for a bit. "Old is when you have gray hair," he finally says, but I can tell as soon as the words come out of his mouth that he isn't satisfied with his response. And then he looks at Dorothy, who is sitting beside him. The octogenarian's hair is completely gray. He covers his face in his hands to hide his embarrassment.

Dorothy pats him on the back and then says to him, "I had a sister who had gray hair when she was nineteen. So to me gray hair doesn't at all mean you're old. And some people with gray hair dye it, so you can't use that as a criterion."

Mark Evans, one of the older folks in attendance, says, "I think the answer to the 'so old' question is the word 'that.' . . ."

"How so?" I ask.

"I might say, I'm so old *that* I have grandchildren," replies Mark, a retired policeman who now is the volunteer director of a regional drug prevention program. "But to me saying something like this is not judgmental. It is not saying that you are in fact old or young. I would not draw any other conclusion from what I said except that I am old enough to have grandchildren. So the word 'that' is a qualifier. I might say, 'I'm so old that I can vote,' or 'I'm so old that I can legally drive a car.' Used in this way, it just means that I'm of an age that opens, or closes, certain possibilities to me—nothing more or less."

Karen Jenkins, another of the older folks, then says, "I'd never thought about it that way before, but I think Mark is right. If I say that I'm old enough that I have a daughter and I'm old enough to be a grandmother, like Mike said, neither of these things means that I'm old or 'so old.' Just like a three-year-old is 'so old' that he can ride a tricycle, I'm 'so old' enough that I have a daughter and granddaughter, or I'm 'so old' that I have had enough rich experiences to write my autobiography—which I'm actually doing! So one way to look at 'so old' is in relation to things we can or can't do or have, and another way is to look at it as a way of determining what we are or aren't yet qualified or able to do or to be."

Christopher Phillips

"From what the young people here have said so far, 'so old' is *ooooooolllldd*," Dorothy says. "It's something that's really dramatic and something we all have to face eventually, and it's not something that all people look forward to. But some people look forward to it. They call it the golden age. Of course, I don't consider myself a senior citizen. I'm a recycled teenager." Everyone, young and old, laughs.

She goes on to say, "My love of learning has never grown old. I still love to take classes and to learn to do new things. In fact, the older I get, the more I want to learn and experience new things. Right now, I'm taking ballroom dance lessons, and I'm learning to speak Chinese so I can volunteer at a center that provides day care for the children of recent Chinese immigrants to the U.S."

What she says brings to mind an encomium Michel de Montaigne once wrote about Socrates: "There is nothing more remarkable in Socrates than the fact that in his old age he finds time to take lessons in dancing and playing instruments, and considers it well spent." Shortly before he died, Montaigne wrote an aphorism that reflects Dorothy's philosophy of old age: "The shorter my possession of life, the deeper and fuller I must make it."

I now look over at Barbara, one of the most loquacious participants at the Socrates Café she regularly attends at a local coffeehouse. Today, she has been uncharacteristically quiet. She has been so rapt in listening to the children that she hasn't said anything herself. "Barbara, what do you think?" I ask.

"It seems like a lot of people don't care to say they're old because they think it's bad to be old," she says after a considerable while. "There's some good things about being old. Dorothy, for instance, is respected because she's old. You might say she's 'so old' that she's highly respected."

"People don't criticize you as much when you're old," she continues. "They think you know more because you're old, so they listen to you. But I'm not sure old people know more. I think you can learn just as much from children, just like I've already learned a great deal from the children here. You just learn different types of things from them than what you'd learn from older people."

She pauses. Then she says in a firm voice, "Trees get older, furniture gets older, keepsakes get older, and they get more precious. That's why people go visit the ancient redwood groves, because they are more precious as they get older. That's why jewelry becomes more precious to us as it 'ages.'"

Then she says. "Everything changes over time. Everything ages. A lot of people think time is an enemy. They don't want things to change. But change is part of life, just as time is."

Many philosophers in the historical canon have indeed seemed to view time and change as an enemy. They believe that time and change are illusory, and that "ultimate reality" is timeless and changeless. For instance, pre-Socratic philosophers such as Pythagoras—who was also a mathematician, mystic, and founder of a religious brotherhood that believed in the immortality and transmigration of the soul—associated perfection with timelessness, and considered change a terrible flaw or blemish. But the second-century A.D. Roman emperor and philosopher Marcus Aurelius, a proponent of the Stoic philosophy who held that death is as natural as birth, wrote that time and change go hand in hand, and that it is "no evil for things to undergo change." Time and change, he believed, are "suitable to universal nature. . . . Dost thou not see that for thyself also to change is just the same, and equally necessary for the universal nature?" Walter

Kaufmann goes a bit further, and maintains that time and change not only are indispensable bedfellows but are artists of a sort. For better or worse, he says, time transforms and transfigures everything: "Time is often destructive—as old sculptors are when they work on a piece of stone. Yet old faces can be much more expressive than young ones, old walls and sculptures much richer than new ones." Nonetheless, time has a destructive bent made especially vivid by Stephen King in *The Green Mile*, whose centenarian narrator Paul Edgecombe was "forced" into a nursing home by his grandchildren. "Time here is like a weak acid that erases first memory and then the desire to go on living," Edgecombe says.

"What do you think about this old and 'so old' stuff?" I say, turning now to Veronica. The reserved nine-year-old so far hasn't said a word. She tugs on both her pigtails as she thinks about what she wants to say.

"Sometimes, when you ask older people a question," she finally says, "you can tell just by what they say that they know more than you. I ask my grandmother lots of questions—for advice or for help with school, things like that—because she is 'so old' that she has a lot of experience."

"What do you mean by experience?" I ask.

"Well, she's learned more than me, she's had a lot more things happen to her, because she's been around so much longer. So she knows more than I do. So if I'm having a problem with a friend, or with something at school, chances are she's been through something like it because she's 'so old' and can give me some good advice based on her experience."

"So you think aging—being 'so old' in the way you're using the term—is in many ways a very good thing?" I ask.

"I do," Veronica replies.

"I do too," says Barbara, "I think that very much. I think that

I'm 'so old' that I enjoy and appreciate things more now than I ever have in my life."

"Like what kinds of things?"

"You appreciate the young people here talking. You appreciate learning what they think. They're more valuable to you. You appreciate knowledge more than you do when you're young. I don't think you recognize the value of things until you get older. I didn't recognize the value of learning until I was 'so old.' I've started taking college classes in ecology and I hope this will help me in my volunteer work as an environmental activist. In fact, who knows . . . I may go on to earn my Ph.D." A few seem to look at her to see if she is kidding, but she clearly is quite serious. Then she says, "I'm not quite sure how to put this, but learning makes me feel young. It makes me very passionate about my life and all the life around me."

In his book *The Third Age*, the sociologist William A. Sadler profiled a woman who, after retiring, returned to college and in her seventies earned a Ph.D.; she now is a recognized scholar, social activist, and much sought-after speaker on aging. The woman told Sadler that even though she had indeed reached the "category of old," she still considered herself "young in many ways," and in many ways a better person "because I have had more experience and I think I have more wisdom." Sadler describes her as "old but not old, young but not young," and speculates that her "confusion" in labeling herself "has prevented her from buying into the conventional meaning of a given age and helped her shape an identity that combines growing older with growing young." He could just as easily have been describing Barbara, and so many of the other older folks taking part in this dialogue.

"Karen?" I say. Karen Jenkins seems to be thinking deeply.

"I'm thinking about that *Fiddler on the Roof* song, 'Sunrise, Sunset,'" Karen says. "It is a song sung by a father who suddenly realizes that his child is a woman, and he hadn't even been aware until that moment that she'd grown up. It happens so fast—like a quantum leap. I'm 'so old' that I've made a quantum leap from being a rather youngish person to being an old person. I'm 'so old,' for instance, that I don't get around so well anymore, and I'm 'so old' that most of my childhood friends have passed away."

She sighs, but then smiles brightly. "And yet, I'm basically the same person inside that I was when I was fifteen," she says. "I've just gained a little more knowledge and experience."

"The body and the mind change over time," Dorothy then says. "You might say they 'age.' But I don't think that has to be the same thing as saying they 'grow old.' Certainly, if you quit having a passion for learning and living, your mind can 'grow old' from disuse—but that can happen at a very young age. But if your mind is constantly nurtured, it can 'grow young' as you age."

"I think that's a beautiful way to put it," says Anna. Until now, the spry and vivacious nonagenarian—who was a first-grade teacher for fifty-eight years, until she retired three years ago and turned her hobby, oil painting, into a full-time pursuit—hasn't spoken. She falls into a silent reverie, smiling to herself, and I think that the demure, reticent woman has said all she has to say. But then she looks at us and says, "I'm starting to think that you not only can 'age gracefully,' but, if you always cultivate your sense of wonder, you can 'age youthfully.'"

WHERE WAS I WHEN I NEEDED ME?

"What am I doing?" I said to myself.

I pulled my car over to the shoulder of the interstate. I turned off the engine. I looked at my hands. They were trembling slightly. I took a deep breath. But I did not move. I stayed parked on the shoulder, paralyzed.

I have embarked on what, for me, is the quintessential journey into the unknown.

It is the midsummer of 1996. I had reached the point where I could no longer bring myself to continue with what had ceased to be a professional life that had meaning for me. My personal life was also fragmented. My wife and I had come to the reluctant realization that if we hoped to salvage a friendship, we would need to end our marriage.

We both had been agonizing for ages over how to make essential changes. I had spent far too long bemoaning all the things I hadn't done, all the time I had wasted. I'd dwelled on questions like: Why had I given up so easily on my aspirations? Why had I failed to follow the path of a different drummer? It was a draining exercise, to torture myself with these questions. And it was a seductive waste of time. It was so easy to stay mired in the past and bemoan all that hadn't been done; so hard to pick oneself up and move forward.

Finally, prayerfully, my Socratic sensibility kicked in. The first order of business was to ask: Am I asking the right questions? Were the questions I'd been beating myself up with the sort of questions that could lead to forward-looking answers that could in turn help me chart a new course for my life?

No way. I wasn't asking fruitful questions. I was asking the kind of introspective past-dwelling questions that would be of no help in making a radical transformation in my life here and now. I began to think up new questions, better questions: What do I really want to do as an avocation or calling? If I resumed being the sublime risk-taker I once was, what calling would make me feel as if I was getting the most out of my mortal moment? What am I *meant* to do?

I remembered once reading a *Rolling Stone* interview with Bono, lead singer of the Irish rock band U2, that gave me considerable pause. In the interview Bono said, "There's a battle . . . between good and evil, and I think you've got to find your place in that. It may be on a factory floor, or it may be writing songs. When you're there—when you're where you should be and you know it in your heart—*that* is when you're involved. . . . I can't change the world, but I can change the world in me."

Similarly, Walter Kaufmann, in his book *The Faith of a Heretic*, recounts reading, when he was seventeen years old and had just escaped from Nazi Germany, a book based on van Gogh's life. He tells how van Gogh planned to live with the miners, descend with them into the pits, and "share their miseries. But Zola told him that it was a 'senseless' act and would in no way help the miners. Zola, who'd written *Germinal*, a novel depicting the abject life of the miners, had helped them much more by making their plight more universally known than van Gogh could ever have done by suffering with them. Indeed, the conditions of the miners improved somewhat, and humanity was elevated somewhat, as a result of *Germinal*." After reading *Germinal*, Kaufmann concluded, "It might be all right to continue college if that would enable me to do some service that I could not do without an education."

Kaufmann's sentiment about finding your unique place and "doing some service" in your unique way is not so different from Bono's. He comes even closer to Bono when he relates, in *From Shakespeare to Existentialism*, the "peculiar piety" of Friedrich Nietzsche and the German poet Rainer Maria Rilke, whose haunting poem "Archaic Torso of Apollo" ends with the injunction "You must change your life." Both Nietzsche and Rilke rejected "all that has hardened into stereotypes . . . in the resolve to be open and ready for their own individual call."

In *The Birth of Tragedy*, Nietzsche wonders what would have happened if Socrates hadn't been open and ready for his individual call. He muses darkly on the "annihilation" that likely would have befallen humankind if Socrates—whom he calls "the turning point ... in world history"—had not cultivated his passion for rational inquiry and employed it in "the service of knowledge."

Despite the noble efforts of Socrates, I'm not sure they represented a turning point in world history. History through the ages has been dominated by accounts of man's atrocities against his fellow man, and the annihilation of which Nietzsche speaks has been an ever-looming prospect. Did Socrates merely postpone the day in which we would slip all the way into the abyss? If so, what does this say of his efforts, and that of all those who have since striven, as Voltaire put it in *Candide*, to "cultivate our garden" by making society more rational and humane?

I had long taken to heart this passage from William James:

> If the generations of mankind suffered and laid down their lives; if martyrs sang in the fire ... for no other end than that a race of creatures of such unexampled insipidity should succeed, and protract ... their contented and inoffensive lives, why, at such a rate ... better ring down the curtain before the last act of the play, so that a business that began so importantly may be saved from so singularly flat a winding up.

This passage haunted me of late. The ethics writer Laurence Shames described America in the 1980s as a place without community or purpose, where success was "defined almost exclusively in terms of money ... without reference to the substance of one's achievement" much less to "high intent," where people "came to believe there didn't have to *be* a purpose," and where ethical lapses were "flagrant and widespread." If anything, this characterization is even more apropos today. In fact, if anything, the pendulum has swung even further away from social responsibility and toward unbridled personal gain. In my journeys across the country as a freelance writer, I had become increasingly disturbed by what I perceived as an extreme and pervasive self-absorption and intolerance among people, coupled with a lack of any sense that they were their brothers' and sisters' keepers. We hadn't just become the "what's in it for me" society; we'd become the "to hell with you" society.

Just as disturbing was a growing sense of pessimistic fatalism and helplessness—a sense that what people said and thought and did no longer mattered much, and that they had little if any control over the circumstances that befell them. In the past, such endemic societal dispositions often were symptoms of more deep-rooted problems that in turn precipitated some of the bleakest periods of human history. But just as there have always been those who've exploited such mass phenomena for the worst of ends, there have also always been people from many walks of life who have endeavored to combat and transcend them.

In trying to formulate and crystallize my own mission in life, I often asked myself: What could I do that would in some modest way further the deeds of those noble souls who had come before me and, as William James put it, "suffered and laid down their lives" to better the lot of humankind? What is my place? What is my service? What am I open to?

When the answer came, it was an epiphany: I wanted be a philosopher in the mold of Socrates. I wanted to hold Socratic dialogues. I wanted to reach out to anyone and everyone who'd like to engage with me in a common quest to gain a better understanding of ourselves and of human nature—and who shared with me the aspiration of becoming more empathetic people and more critical and creative philosophical inquirers. The answer was so obvious that it also quickly became obvious why I hadn't dared to ask the question before. Because once I answered it honestly, I knew I would have to ask the next critical question, one fraught with dizzying change: Why can't I advance in the direction of my dreams, right now, regardless of how much time I feel I've wasted?

Then it hit me: it was all too easy to stay in this rut of bemoaning time wasted and wallowing in misery. But the hard work of making needed changes that would put my life back on what I felt would be a meaningful track required a new set of questions: What precisely can I do to realize my dreams? What steps do I have to take? What sacrifices will I have to make? Am I willing to make them?

Frightened as I was at the prospect of dramatically changing my life, I was ready. Or, at least, I thought I was. But it is one thing to formulate a plan and express your intention to carry it out. It is quite another to turn thought into deed.

But that is what I was doing now—or was on the verge of doing—as I sat in my car along the roadside. I'd read about philosophers in Europe who were holding philosophy discussions with the public at cafés. And I'd read about a disillusioned former Columbia University philosophy professor, Matthew Lipman, who was attempting to breathe new life into philosophy with the "Philosophy for Children" program he founded at Montclair State University in Upper Montclair, New Jersey. Lipman's admirable aim was to introduce Philosophy for Children curricula at schools and form what he characterized as "classroom communities of philosophical inquiry." In his seminal *Thinking and Education*, Lipman criticized the "overspecialized mind" as "the bane of academic life." He advocated a return to a type of philosophy that encourages thinking in, about, and among the disciplines, arguing that "what goes on at the seams and creases among the disciplines is at least as important as what goes on within them." Like the café philosophers in Europe, Lipman was attempting to rejuvenate a discipline they'd deemed ossified and irrelevant.

Both approaches excluded those who couldn't or didn't go to school, or weren't able to visit a café to engage in philosophical inquiry. And they seemed to use a hodgepodge of methods of inquiry—or no spelled-out method at all. Many café philosophers in Europe seemed to be unabashed *anti*-academics. Most notably, the late Marc Sautet, a Nietzsche scholar who earned his doctorate at the Sorbonne, believed academic philosophers had mortgaged their philosophical birthright. Sautet railed against the "academic ghettoization" of philosophy in the universities, and he went on to catalyze a *café philo* movement.

Though I, too, was critical of many aspects of the ivory tower, academic philosophy in particular, I nonetheless felt it had a rightful place and a potentially noble calling. To be sure, as Matthew Lipman wrote, with their "archaic programs, their bemused bureaucracies, and their instructors indifferent to matters of pedagogy," the universities have all too often shirked their calling and largely been unresponsive to constructive criticism both from within and without their cloister.

But even with its shortcomings, I think higher education has been much more of a boon than a bane. And over the last generation, thanks largely to the burgeoning public university system, it is within the reach of more and more—so much so that many take it as almost their birthright that they'll continue their education at a university after secondary school. All the more reason, I think, to fight the good fight and work to make the universities paradigms of creative and rigorous learning, rather than abandon them altogether.

My hope was to engage in a sort of philosophical outreach that would, among other things, help resuscitate scholarly philosophy by expanding greatly both the subject matter that could be grist for philosophical inquiry and the audience to be engaged. And I wanted to build bridges between academia and the so-called outside world.

Elementary and secondary schools are also magnets for criticism. "The alarm bells of American education sound the woes of fragile knowledge and poor thinking," according to David Perkins, director of Harvard Project Zero, one of the foremost centers for children's learning, and a professor at the Harvard Graduate School of Education. In *Smart Schools: Better Thinking and Learning for Every Child*, Perkins says that the United States, by and large, lacks "smart schools"—schools that are "informed, energetic and thoughtful" and that have "demanding goals." As a result, he says, we are "unable to compete efficiently with other nations that have their acts together better." Perkins' criticisms are far from unique among advocates of public school reform. But as with higher education, the impassioned discussion is framed around the quality of education that our children and youth deserve, not around whether we should dispense with schools or schooling. Critics of our nation's schools often overlook the fact that there are dedicated and progressive educators throughout the country who are making marked inroads in implementing curricula that raise the bar of academic standards children are expected to meet, and that inspire and challenge children to become more critical and conscientious thinkers.

As with higher education, I hoped to do my singular part to bring about much-needed changes in our nation's schools. But in philosophizing with children, I didn't aspire to develop yet another curriculum for overtaxed teachers or supplant traditional school curricula—in fact, I had no interest in using any sort of curricula at all. I wanted to philosophize *with* children in the same way, using the same method, I would with adults. By operating on the edges of the traditional school sphere—by holding

Philosophers Clubs both during and after school—I hoped to enhance and complement what schools were doing. And by instilling children with that critical "fourth R," namely reasoning, I hoped they'd be motivated more than ever to learn the traditional three Rs of reading, writing, and arithmetic. But I also hoped they'd be inspired to become probing, expert questioners who weren't cowed by anyone who tried to curb their curiosity. If this hope could be realized, I firmly felt that this generation of children would be our best hope of making the dramatic changes necessary to make both our schools and our universities ever-evolving laboratories of creative and critical cross-disciplinary learning that seek to promote imaginative vision and rational thinking.

Still, my ultimate goal was to extend philosophical outreach far beyond schools and universities and cafés. I believed that if we were ever going to make our society more participatory, more democratic, then everyone had to feel he or she had a stake in the process. Everyone had to know in no uncertain terms that what he or she say and think and do matters and counts. Only then would people from all walks of life be inspired to articulate their worldview and expand their horizons by engaging in the complementary pursuits of knowledge and human excellence.

I had packed my belongings and left our home hours earlier. Every step of the way to my new home in New Jersey, where I planned to set up shop, I considered turning back. As I drove, the impulse to turn back grew stronger. Finally, I'd pulled off the road. I could not go on. I could not go back either.

"What am I doing?" I said, my hands still gripped tight to the steering wheel.

I had been repeating this question mantra-like without realizing it.

I felt lost in a numbing way—a stranger to myself with no

idea who I was, what I wanted. I felt as if I had abandoned myself at the moment when I needed myself most.

An hour passed. Finally, somewhere inside, a voice well buried beneath mountains of doubt managed to make itself heard: "You're moving in the direction of your dreams."

I pulled out a crumpled piece of paper from my pocket. It was something I had carried with me for years, a section of a page from a careworn paper on which was printed a quote from Johann Wolfgang von Goethe, the great German Romantic poet, novelist, and scientist—a truly Socratic inquisitor of the late nineteenth century. On the piece of paper were these words from Goethe: "Until one is committed, there is hesitancy, the chance to draw back, always ineffectiveness. Concerning all acts of initiative and creation, there is one elementary truth the ignorance of which kills countless ideas and splendid plans: the moment one definitely commits oneself, then . . . a whole stream of events issues from the decision, raising in one's favor all manner of unforeseen incidents and meetings and material assistance which no man could have dreamed would have come his way. Whatever you can do, or dream you can do, begin it. Boldness has genius, power and magic in it. Begin it now."

I folded the piece of paper back up and put it in my pocket. I put a pad of paper in the passenger seat and I wrote in capital letters with a red magic marker what I would do soon after arriving in New Jersey: (1) Start public philosophy discussion groups at cafés and coffeehouses, at nursing homes and senior centers, at schools and day care centers, at community centers and jails and hospices—wherever people yearn to inquire philosophically; (2) Begin now.

For the first time, I realized that there was no turning back. For the first time, my understandable fears and doubts served to magnify just how critical it was that I continue on to New Jersey. For the first time, I realized just how much I needed *me*, and that if

I dared to turn back now, I would be abandoning myself in an almost unforgivable way.

I turned the ignition. I pulled back onto the interstate.

I was on my way.

Christopher
Phillips

WHAT'S LOVE GOT TO DO WITH IT?

It is 7 P.M., time for Socrates Café to begin, and no one has showed.

This is just the second week since I started a new Socrates Café in Montclair, New Jersey. A few people came to the initial gathering the previous Tuesday. But this week it looks like I have an empty house.

These things take time, I tell myself, as I sit on the stool like Rodin's *Thinker*. Still, I am feeling out of sorts. I wonder whether I am wasting my time, whether it is silly or even foolhardy to try to revive the spirit and ethos of Socrates. Nagging, negative thoughts creep in: People are too busy, too self-involved, too sure they know the answer, to want to engage with others in Socratic give-and-take. If someone had predicted at that low moment that in just ten weeks upwards of forty people would begin to cram into this coffeehouse each Tuesday night to philosophize with me, and that this event would soon generate a flurry of national media attention, I would've told him he was crazy.

Five minutes later a woman comes in. She pauses just past the entrance and sees me sitting on a stool. I must look kind of silly sitting on it, since no one else is in sight (the owners are in the kitchen at the moment). It looks like she's thinking of turning right back around and leaving. But she doesn't. At least, not yet. "Is this the Socrates Café?" she asks me.

"Yes," I reply. "It looks like it's just you and me."

She smiles, her temples crinkling in the most captivating way. She has long black hair and warm brown eyes. She has so much natural color in her face that it would be a crime if she wore makeup. She is wearing a hand-stitched white cotton dress with beautifully intricate embroidery.

She decides to stay. I get off the stool and we take a seat at a table.

"Did you have any particular question in mind that you wanted to talk about?" I ask.

She hesitates for a moment before replying. Then she says, "Well, yes, I do have a question."

I wait.

She hesitates a while longer. She is fingering the napkin on the table and seems to have momentarily forgotten about me. Finally she lifts her head and looks at me.

"What is love?" she asks.

"What is love?" It's all I can think of to say right off the top of my head. She doesn't reply. We both sit in awkward silence.

Finally I say, "Socrates professed relative ignorance in all areas of knowledge—except love. In Plato's *Lysis*, he says, 'While I may be worthless in all other matters, I've somehow been given by a god the talent to recognize easily a lover and a beloved.'"

"In Plato's *Symposium*," she replies, "Socrates says, 'I don't see how I can refuse to speak on the subject of love, since I have no knowledge at all other than that of matters concerning love.'"

She sees the look of surprise on my face and smiles. "The *Symposium* is one of my favorite of Plato's dialogues," she says. "To me it's as beautiful as Shakespeare's sonnets."

I smile in turn and go on to say to this enigmatic woman, "I guess I should admit that I'm at extreme odds with Socrates on this subject: I feel I can speak with much more confidence about virtually anything else other than love. But if we're going to have a dialogue on love, it'd probably be wise to raise the same sorts of questions Socrates did. When he examined the question 'What is love?' he felt it could only be answered if you understood its nature and its works."

Christopher Phillips

"I really like where Socrates says in the *Symposium* that love, or eros, links the sublime to the mundane, and gives human life meaning," she says. "I agree with Socrates that love is the longing of the soul for beauty. I like this because he isn't describing love in any sort of static way. He's giving it a sublime function and purpose."

In early Greek thought, love was considered predominantly sexual in nature, and Eros was the Greek god of erotic love. Eventually, due largely to the work of Plato, the concept of love was expanded and refined. Plato considered love the pervasive "force" in all human actions and compulsions, and eros came to represent many manifestations of love. Plato's Socrates said that love starts with a particular person as its object, leading to a physical relationship between two people. This love, however, is eventually sublimated and directed toward the beauty within a particular person. But as the woman with whom I am engaged in dialogue said so eloquently, Plato made clear in the *Symposium* that even this manifestation of eros is just a way station to ever higher forms of love—love of humankind, love of all truth and beauty, love of the perfect form of beauty, which transcends reality. Near the end of the *Symposium,* Diotima says that love is not something that can just be defined in a flourish of fine words, but must be seen and felt and imagined and experienced. Though a lifelong loner, Charles Sanders Peirce, a renowned American philosopher of science and language, believed he experienced this sublime form of eros—this lasting union with aesthetic forms—that Diotima described. Peirce said that when he undertook his philosophical investigations, he was "animated by a true eros."

After a considerable pause, the young woman says to me, "Love is a response. Love is something to be expressed, to be demonstrated, and it leads to this sublime place that is within us but also transcends us. But this place is very, very hard to reach."

"Amen," I say, more to myself than to her.

We spend much of the next two hours attempting to throw our arms around that most profound and yet hard-to-fathom concept, love. Throughout, I am having trouble concentrating, or at least I seem to hover in and out of the conversation. At some point I mention how my own response to love has all too often been to run away from it, or at the very least to keep it at arm's length. But as we continue to talk, I find myself thinking that there are also times when love cannot be fended off and it envelops you.

Her name is Cecilia Chapa. She is from Mexico City. It turns out she is a student at the local university. She is studying to earn her master's degree in education. She already has a bachelor's degree in philosophy and she tells me that one day she hopes in her own way to do something similar to what I am doing and bring philosophy back "to the people." The previous year, she was a teacher at a school for indigenous children in Chiapas, Mexico, a rural state in the remote, impoverished southern region of the country where the Zapatistas have long been waging guerrilla warfare to stymie further efforts by the government to exploit indigenous tribes. After earning her master's degree, she plans to devote her life to working with underprivileged children, helping them help themselves by cultivating in them the critical and creative thinking skills they will need if they are to empower themselves and their communities. She says she believes with all her heart that children are our future and our salvation.

We fall silent after a while. I watch her as she nurses the cup of tea, now cold, that she ordered two hours earlier. She is smiling to herself. Then, looking directly at me, she says, "My favorite part of Plato's *Symposium* is the speech by Aristophanes."

It is a favorite of mine too. And like a child who never tires of hearing his favorite bedtime story, I listen raptly as Cecilia says, "Plato tells a story—I guess what most people would call a myth, but I'm not sure if I agree—that the sexes were not originally two, as they are now. There used to be three: man, woman, and Androgynous, the union of the two. These sexes were round and had four hands and four feet and one head with two faces. To curb what he felt was the growing arrogance and might of the human race, Zeus cut each of these three sexes in half. And from then on, the two severed parts desired their other half. They threw their arms around one another at every opportunity and longed more than anything to be one again."

Then Cecilia says, "Wait, I want to read this part of the passage verbatim, because it's so beautiful. She retrieves from her purse a copy of Plato's dialogues that is beyond dog-eared. She quickly thumbs to the page she's looking for and reads, "And when one of them meets with his other half, the actual half of himself . . . the pair are lost in an amazement of love and friendship and intimacy, and will not be out of the other's sight even for a moment: these are the people who pass their whole lives together." She stops reading there, even though the speech continues. She eventually closes the book and puts it away. She looks downward as she smoothes the folds of her dress. Then she looks at me with a smile that I can only describe as wonderfully disturbing and mysterious.

I believe that it is at this point in our long conversation that it dawns on me that I want to ask her, "How do you know when you're in love?"

But I do not ask her. Not then. I wait until nearly two years later, after we're already married.

I V

What's It All About?

I am and always have been one of those natures
who must be guided by reflective questioning.

—SOCRATES

REMEMBRANCE OF
PHILOSOPHIZING PAST

**Christopher
Phillips**

"Do we philosophize as much as we used to?"

Patricia, a vibrant woman in her late seventies can't even wait for me to take my perch on the stool before she poses this question. As usual, we are gathered in the community room of an unadorned red brick housing complex for low-income senior citizens in northern New Jersey. Once a month or so, on Friday afternoons, I have been facilitating Socrates Café there. The residents are a diverse and contentious and thoughtful group, imbued with the Socratic spirit. They challenge and inspire and exasperate me and one another—and we love each other dearly. The community room is a bright, pleasant room with lots of natural sunlight filtering in. The residents sit around small round tables covered with patterned tablecloths and decorated with vases of silk flowers, drinking coffee and eating cookies. It is almost as if we were at a café.

"What do you mean?" I ask Patricia after I settle on top of my stool, which one of the residents has brought from her apartment for me to use.

"I wonder whether we philosophize as much as those of old," Patricia says in a lilting voice. "For instance, those who wrote the Declaration of Independence seemed to philosophize a great deal. But today, politicians don't philosophize at all. In fact, hardly anyone seems to philosophize anymore. Or at least, they don't philosophize *well*."

"Well, before we can answer that question, maybe we first need to pin down what philosophizing is," I say. "William James thought something to the effect that philosophizing was a critique of common sense. And what I think he meant is: We should take a hard look at the concepts that we use every day and think we use clearly—that we think we all understand and see eye to eye on—and see if they really are as clear and rational as we think they are, or if there's more, or less, to them than meets the eye."

No one says a word in reply and I'm a bit concerned I may not have been very clear myself. But Patricia comes to my rescue. "Why don't we use William James' definition of philosophizing as a way of answering my question," she suggests. "Let's look at some of the concepts used in the Declaration and see if they really were used as clearly and rationally as the Founding Fathers thought."

"That's a wonderful idea," I say, and see that most of the others are nodding in agreement. "Let's take the part of the sentence in the Declaration that says: 'We hold these truths to be self-evident, that all men are created equal.' Do you think a great deal of 'good philosophizing' went into the construction of that phrase?"

Janice, colorfully garbed in a dress patterned with multicolored flowers and wearing a feathered hat that on anyone else would look gaudy, stands up, as is her habit before speaking. Supporting herself with the tips of her fingers on the surface of the table in front of her, she says, "I don't know how much philosophizing went into writing that sentence. But however much it was, it wasn't *good* philosophizing. Because it's not true that we're all created equal. We all take up different space, we all have different experiences, we all have different talents. None of us has equal chances at happiness, none of us has equally good health, none of us has equal opportunities. So we might all be created *equally*—we're all born in the same way, from a mother's womb—but we are not all created *equal.*"

A frail but energetic woman with a very sober countenance who is seated at the same table as Janice says, "I don't think we're all created equally even in the way Janice is speaking. Some children are born to malnourished moms. Some are born to moms and dads who smoke or do drugs. Some are 'crack' babies. Some are born after complicated pregnancies that do irreparable damage to them."

A pleasant, dapperly dressed man with a handlebar mustache that he regularly twists and tugs says, "I think the sentence 'All men are created equal' is cynical. What it meant was that all well-to-do white men were created equal. No one else had any rights. So, because they didn't have a real cross section of people from the colonies help form the Declaration of Independence, they philosophized about the concept 'equal' in a way that still allowed for slavery, among other glaring inequalities. The Founding Fathers were masters of what equal meant, so they were masters of who was equal and who wasn't."

Patricia then says, "Now I'm beginning to wonder whether the Founding Fathers really were as good at philosophizing as I'd thought. The more I listen to what the others here are saying, the more I think they philosophized just as badly as people do today."

"Well, let's not judge them so quickly," I say. "I think we need to look at the Declaration that was produced in the context of their time. I think most would agree that what they wrote was an extraordinarily progressive and even courageous document."

The view that all men are equal did not originate with the Declaration. The English materialist and empiricist Thomas Hobbes, one of the founders of modern political philosophy, developed in his famous work *Leviathan*, published in 1651, a "philosophy of natural equality" in which all men by nature are equal in physical and mental capacities. Not that they possess the exact same degree of mental and physical ability in every regard, but, according to Hobbes, the deficiencies of each in one area are compensated for in others. This view strongly influenced subsequent moral and political philosophy. In his *Tractatus Theologico-Politicus*, published in

1670, Baruch Spinoza wrote that a democracy is "of all forms of government the most natural and the most consonant with individual liberty" because "all men remain equals, as they were in the state of nature." In 1690 the English philosopher John Locke, the highly influential founder of British empiricism, set forth his political theory in *Two Treatises of Government*, in which he argued that men are, "by nature, all free, equal and independent." The Swiss-born French thinker Jean-Jacques Rousseau echoed these ideas in his book *The Social Contract*, published in 1762; this work had a huge impact on political philosophy, as well as on educational theory and the Romantic movement. Rousseau implies in the opening passage that all men are equal when he states that "man is born free." Indeed, soon after the book's publication, the writers of the constitution of Massachusetts took Rousseau's passage and made clear what he implied: "All men are born free and equal, and have certain natural, essential and unalienable rights." The Declaration of Independence made this philosophy of equality even more explicit by holding man's condition of freedom and equality to be a "self-evident" truth. It is one thing to philosophize about equality, but making this notion the cornerstone of a nation, as the Founding Fathers did, was indeed progressive and courageous—even if word did not always match deed. While Thomas Jefferson, who wrote the Declaration, was himself a slaveholder who believed in capital punishment, his words gave future generations the ammunition they needed to strive to make the Declaration live up to its billing.

"Let's take the second half of the passage I quoted from in the Declaration, where the Founding Fathers also hold it to be self-evident that all men 'are endowed by their Creator with certain unalienable Rights; that among these are Life, Liberty, and the pursuit of Happiness,'" I say to the Socrates Café participants. "Even if at times they weren't consistent in the application of the concepts in such passages, wasn't this a huge step forward in terms of human rights?"

Janice stands up again. With a somewhat peevish gesture, she says, "I think this passage is a clever bit of philosophizing. It implies that while we all had equal rights to pursue happiness, there was no guarantee that any of us would attain it. If we were all created equal, like they said we were, it would seem that if one of us attains happiness, the rest of us would too. But that's not really the way it is."

"I'm starting to wonder if happiness even matters!" says Patricia. She seems surprised that she is thinking such a thing. Then she says, "There's things more important than happiness. First you have to have enough food on the table for yourself and your family. You have to have good health. I think these things are more important than happiness."

"I think happiness is important," says a stooped, wizened man who until now has seemed preoccupied by his own thoughts and has not said a word. "But what's important is that you do not infringe in a bad way on others while pursuing happiness."

"How do you keep people from infringing on others in a 'bad way'?" I ask.

"There are laws on the books so that we have to keep our bad compulsions in check," he says. "I think this was a needed constraint on our liberties that the Founding Fathers put in the Constitution. So the Founding Fathers did philosophize well, I think, when they came up with this passage."

The type of liberty of which he speaks—liberty to do anything you choose without constraint—is what Hobbes in *Leviathan* called "natural liberty." For Hobbes, just as with the Founding Fathers, this was a liberty well worth dispensing with. Hobbes believed the state of nature, in which one can do whatever one pleases without impediment, is a state of perpetual strife that pits every person against everyone else. Wrote Hobbes: "Where there is no common power, there is no law: where no law, no injustice." Hobbes believed such liberty was a negative liberty that needed to be replaced by "civil liberty," the type of liberty you gain when you leave the state of nature and form a commonwealth. Hobbes was considered a heretic by the Church of England for his defense of the independence of religious life. He believed that only a social contract preserves one from the "war of every man against every man" that constitutes the natural state, in which the life of man is "nasty, solitary, brutish, and short."

Another participant eventually says, "I wonder where you draw the line between laws that curb your ability to act on certain compulsions and laws that are so restrictive that government becomes sort of 'Big Brother.'"

Rachel, the energetic young program director at the senior residence, then says, "I don't eat meat because I don't think it's humane. But I respect the right of others to do so. I would never want to be 'Big Brother' about it and force them to do as I do."

"Hmmm," I say. "If you are morally opposed to eating meat because you think it's inhumane, can you honestly say it doesn't bother you that others do?"

"Yes," she says hesitantly.

"So what do you think about the laws that now require you to wear seat belts while in a moving vehicle?" I ask her.

"I think each individual should be able to decide whether or not to wear a seat belt," she says.

Then eighty-five-year-old Helena, who was actively involved in the civil rights movement, turns to Rachel, her arms akimbo, and says, "Is that so?"

Rachel no longer looks so certain. "I think so," she says at last.

Wagging a finger at her, Helena then says, "If you don't wear a seat belt, you're putting your life at greater risk. You're endangering your life, and you're showing that you aren't responsibly minded in terms of those you love, in terms of those—like us—who depend on you. If you don't wear your seat belt when you drive, it's like you're saying you're willing to put yourself more at risk and you're willing to put all of us who depend on you at more risk. What does this say about what you think about your life? And what does this say about what you think of us?"

This gives Rachel pause. "I'd never thought of it that way before," she says. "I think you're right." Then she adds with much emotion, "Please don't worry! I always wear my seat belt."

Helena walks over to her and gives her a hug. "We know you love us, honey," she says, patting Rachel's back.

"What happens when we philosophize?" I eventually ask. "What did the creators of the Declaration do that constitutes philosophizing?"

"They engaged in an exchange of ideas," says Clara, a buoyant woman with beautiful long white hair who immigrated decades ago to the United States from Cuba to escape the Castro regime. "But not only did they exchange ideas, they applied their ideas once they reached some sort of consensus."

"I think they could have used our help in writing that Declaration," says Helena. This meets with a chorus of agreement.

Then Janice says, "It seems to me that they needed Socrates to help them write that Declaration."

"Why Socrates?" I ask.

"Because he would have made them examine the key concepts they used in the Declaration with greater care. So they'd have known if the concepts really were, as William James said, as 'clear and rational' as they thought they were—or if there was 'more to them than meets the eye.'"

"I don't know about Socrates," says Patricia, "but they sure needed us!"

THE PHILOSOPHIC SPIRIT

In *How Philosophy Uses Its Past*, John Herman Randall, Jr., equates philosophizing with "a characterization and criticism of the fundamental beliefs involved in all the great enterprises of human culture, science, art, religion, the moral life, social and political activity"—particularly those beliefs that conflict with "inherited knowledge and wisdom." No one embraced the task of examining and critiquing the received wisdom of his time as sweepingly and exhaustively as did Plato. He wrote his dialogues in the midst of a chaotic Athenian landscape in which the *polis*, or city-state, recently had been defeated in the Peloponnesian War, which had lasted nearly thirty years. Before the war, Athens had experienced a period of unbridled prosperity along with a cultural renaissance, but it now seemed to doubt its own credentials. It is in this climate that Plato, around age twenty, is generally believed to have met Socrates. Plato fast became mesmerized by his newfound mentor's singular moral character and passionate intellectual quest for knowledge about how to become a virtuous person, and soon after, he reputedly vowed to follow in Socrates' footsteps and devote his own life to philosophy.

Even though democracy had been restored in Athens after a period of oligarchy, Socrates made many enemies in high places with his unflinching questioning. His trial for heresy, and subsequent conviction and death sentence, left Plato deeply disillusioned with Athens' powers that be, as his subsequent writings showed. John Herman Randall noted that Plato "viewed, and made his readers view, the problems and the chief figures of the period of Athenian prosperity and uncritical self-confidence with something of the cold and fishy eye with which, say, Englishmen have come to regard the booming times of the Age of Kipling and Empire."

Moreover, Plato was so moved by Socrates' death that he apparently felt it his duty to bear witness to him for posterity, making him what would become the paradigmatic figure not just of Western philosophy but also in many ways of human aspiration at its best. In Walter Kaufmann's words, Plato's dialogues, in their haunting portrayals of Socrates, "spurn the safety of a sluggish intellectual and moral imagination" and teach us "impatience with confusions" and instill us with "the passion to reflect." They challenge your perspective at every turn. It is impossible to emerge from reading them unscathed and unchanged.

KNOW THYSELF AT THINE OWN RISK

It is now months since I inaugurated Socrates Café. I have since relocated our philosophical confab to a coffeehouse in Montclair, New Jersey. The establishment, situated along a busy thoroughfare in the old downtown area of the small, ethnically diverse city, is the size of a large master bedroom. I relocated here because of its easy accessibility to so many people from so many walks of life. In the coffeehouse, the outside world seems worlds removed. Shelves are filled with books and magazines for patrons to read. The walls are covered with postmodern paintings. Classical guitar music wafts through stereo speakers. It is the perfect place to wax philosophical till the wee hours. Indeed, Socrates Café at this independently owned coffeehouse is now a weekly staple for about fifty denizens of the region.

On this evening, the discussion has just ended. The question of the night was "How do you know when you know yourself?"

"You can only really know yourself through crisis," says Jim Taylor near the end of the dialogue. This is the third time in the course of the dialogue that Jim, president of a thriving public relations firm, has made this same point, and each time he seems less and less convincing, and less convinced.

"Can't people who lead mundane lives know themselves too?" I ask him. "Can't you know yourself just as well, if not better, through the more regular or even mundane circumstances in your life than through the crises that occur?"

Jim, impeccably dressed as always, his countenance sober as always, adjusts his tie and fiddles with the Windsor knot, even though it is perfectly in place. He habitually does this before responding, not just to buy time but because this is what he does while thinking. "I don't think so," he says at last. "I think you only really become aware of who you are and what you're all about, what you're capable or incapable of, during a time of crisis. Because you put yourself 'to the test' in a crisis."

"But don't you also put yourself to the test in times that have nothing to do with a crisis?" I press him. "Doesn't how you live your everyday 'mundane' life provide the greatest barometer of who you are, and doesn't it also put you to the test in its own way?"

"I think they both do," he concludes. "I think crises make you aware of parts of yourself that you'd never know about otherwise. But I also agree that the way I approach and live each day is instructive of who I am. The thing is, though, that I don't think most of us ever put much thought into who we are, into examining who we are, except in crisis."

"Maybe," I say. "But maybe we're moving a bit too fast. I think we have to explore what a crisis is. Seems to me that living a mundane life can be a type of crisis, a long-term crisis. So I'm not even sure we're talking about two separate things. At least, I think part of knowing ourselves is knowing what type of crisis, if any, we're living or experiencing at the moment."

Only by engaging with Jim did I come to the realization, to the discovery, that I thought of the notion of crisis in this way.

Then Martha asks, "When Socrates said, 'Know thyself,' do you think he knew what a self is and what knowing is?" Martha is forever pushing her somewhat outlandish-looking gold-framed prescription glasses back up the bridge of her nose. I've never known her to offer an answer to any topic we've ever discussed—except, as tonight, an answer in the form of a provocative question.

Christopher
Phillips

"I'm not sure if he ever defined either term explicitly," says Ricki, a poet who has seemed until now either lost in thought or as if she had decided that this conversation was not for her. "But I think he came to know himself by engaging with others in discussions like this."

Then she says, "I don't think a self is something that can be defined, but can only be revealed. Our self is who we are, what we say, what we do. Our self is a perspective, an approach, a disposition, not a thing. It is a work in progress."

I almost wish I could say that we defined precisely what a self is by the end of this discussion. But of course we didn't, though we do at times arrive at some tentative answers. I think many people leave the discussion feeling that they are less sure than ever of how well, or even whether, they know themselves. Tim, a painting contractor, comes up to me after the session and says, "I'm starting to wonder now if there even is such a thing as a self."

"In Plato's *Gorgias*," I say, "Socrates says, 'It would be better for me that my lyre or a chorus were out of tune and loud with discomfort, and that most men should not agree with me, rather than that I, being one, should be out of tune with myself or contradict myself.' I think that one thing he meant by this 'being one' is that he believed he was related to a self, and that this self wasn't just some illusion or some sort of fanciful thinking on his part. What I get from this is that although Socrates felt he could escape the company of others when he wanted to, his self was something he couldn't escape from, even if he'd wanted to."

This doesn't seem to soothe Tim in the least. He says, "I wonder if he just *wanted* to feel this way, because it would be too disturbing to think that maybe there is no self to escape from." And with this jarring thought, he leaves the café.

I notice just then that an extremely tall young man with sharp, angular features, a sallow complexion, and intense blue eyes has been standing just behind me and listening to my brief conversation with Tim.

It is now 10:30 P.M. and, uncharacteristically, I don't feel like tarrying any longer and chatting with anyone else. For reasons I don't understand completely, I feel quite drained. I can see he wants to have a word with me, and I try my best to hide my displeasure at being waylaid. Without saying a word, he just starts shaking my hand. He did not say a word during the discussion. Finally, while still shaking my hand, he says, "If we'd had discussions like this at my university, I'd soon have a Ph.D. in philosophy."

Without prompting, he goes on to tell me that until last month he was a student in a Ph.D. program in philosophy at a university in the Midwest. "I've almost finished writing my dissertation," he says. "But it's a piece of shit. I'm throwing it in the trash." His eyes have a faraway look. But then he looks at me and says, "It's ironic that your topic tonight was on the self, since I was writing my dissertation on the difference between the real self and the imagined self. But it was written in academic mumbo jumbo. I'm sure my professors would've loved it, but I hated myself while I wrote it. I came to know my real self well enough to know that being an academic philosophy professor was not the type of philosopher I wanted to be. In fact, I came to the conclusion that most of them aren't philosophers at all. They imagine themselves to be philosophers, but they aren't real philosophers. I think what some of them do under the guise of philosophy is criminal."

I consider whether I should try to talk him out of his decision to trash his dissertation, but before I have a chance to get a word in edgewise, he tells me, "I'd been toying with the idea of tossing it in the trash for quite a while. But this discussion tonight has given me the resolve really to trash it once and for all. I want to be like Socrates."

"What do you mean?" I ask him, all the while reflecting on the fact that Socrates never wrote a dissertation, never published anything, because he never strove to be a scholastic who committed to advancing a certain thesis.

"It's not just that academics write in jargon," he replies. "The worst thing is that most that I know are timid conformists. I think this is sacrilege. They have the rare privilege of having unheard-of job security, of being almost completely autonomous. So you'd think if anyone would be paradigms of Socratic rigor, it would be university professors. But instead they're almost all anti-Socratic scholastics who write lengthy tomes on small subjects. And they rarely if ever challenge the accepted wisdom of their time."

"But can't you stay in academia and be 'like Socrates'?" I ask him. "One might argue that the easiest thing in the world for you to do would be to abandon ship. But if you really have a vision of what academia can be, if you really aspire to be a Socratic teacher, why don't you stay within the bounds of academia and fight the good fight?"

This gives him pause. "I don't know . . ."

"Why throw away all your years of training?" I tell him. "I can understand why you'd throw away your dissertation. But instead of throwing away your career, why don't you start over? Why

don't you write the kind of dissertation that you think would make Socrates proud? That might take a lot more chutzpah than simply to quit."

I go on to tell him that in addition to all my philosophical outreach activities, I am tapping into the academic world in a creative way that is enabling me to exploit its strengths and helping to make me an even more adept philosophical inquirer in the mold of Socrates. (In fact, I will eventually wind up with three master's degrees: in the humanities, in the natural sciences, and in teaching.)

This seems to give him even more pause. At long last he says, "I think I have a lot more thinking to do." He turns and walks out the door without so much as saying good-bye.

I have no idea what has become of him. He was only in town that one evening, visiting a friend, and he never returned to Socrates Café. I think of him often. Like me, it seems that he discovered who he was by first discovering who he most definitely was not.

SOCRATIC SPIRITS

I began reading philosophy autodidactically as a twelve-year old, when I first became entranced by the Socrates of Plato's dialogues. Socrates never seemed larger than life to me, but rather someone who felt he could always become more than he was at any given time. He seemed to strive always to become "larger," more expansive, daring to push the envelope in terms of his capacity to become a "more excellent" human being. Soon after I first discovered him for myself, I made a sincere but rather inchoate vow to "be like Socrates." But I never seemed to get around to putting word into deed.

Christopher
Phillips

While an undergraduate college student, I took a number of philosophy courses. I was disappointed to no end that my professors did not encourage their students to see ourselves as coinquirers who were there to engage with the professors in the types of impassioned dialogues Socrates and his cohorts held. They tended to treat philosophy like a museum piece that only they, the experts, could discuss with authority. All too often they employed an inaccessible jargon that left students intimidated and bewildered, and vowing never again to take another philosophy course once they had satisfied their degree requirements.

The Canadian novelist and essayist John Ralston Saul, who earned his Ph.D. at King's College London, wrote in his mordantly incisive *Voltaire's Bastards: The Dictatorship of Reason in the West* that one of the "most successful discoveries" of today's academic is that he "could easily defend his territory by the simple development of a specialized language incomprehensible to nonexperts.

> The example of philosophy actually verges on comedy. Socrates, Descartes, Bacon, Locke and Voltaire did not write in a specialized dialect. . . . [T]hey wrote for the general reader of their day. Their language is clear, eloquent and often both moving and amusing. . . . This means that almost anyone with a decent pre-university level education can still pick up Bacon or Descartes, Voltaire or Locke and read them with both ease and pleasure. Yet even a university graduate is hard pressed to make his way through interpretations of these same thinkers by leading contemporary intellectuals. Why, then, would anyone bother trying to read these modern obscurings of the original clarity? The answer is that contemporary universities use these interpretations as the expert's road into the original. The dead philosophers are thus treated as if they were amateurs, in need of expert explanation and protection.

While today's academic elite ballyhoo their "Socratic heritage" at every opportunity, Saul holds that "the way they teach" is the antithesis of the Socratic way. "In the Athenian's case every answer raised a question. With the contemporary elites every question produces an answer."

Saul's commentary tends to reflect much of my undergraduate experience with academic philosophy, and, from what I have gathered over the years, that of many others. However, I've also met many people who were instilled with a lifelong love of philosophy after being inspired by professors who engaged them in a decidedly Socratic way. And even based just on my own college experience, I think Saul overgeneralizes. In my university's government department, I discovered a number of keen-minded professors whose forte was political philosophy and who spoke in simple but by no means simplistic lay language about the great political philosophers both past and present. They treated philosophy as an eminently relevant and vibrant discipline. Best of all, they did indeed employ a version of the Socratic method to engage with us in dialogue. Rather than try to drill in us "the right answer," they tried to help us learn for ourselves that there may be many possible "right answers," but that it was up to us to support our views with cogent, logical, well-supported reasons. Still, Arthur Schopenhauer, the great nineteenth-century German philosopher and prose writer who worked outside the academic mainstream, was no doubt correct in his assessment that "very few philosophers have ever been professors of philosophy, and even fewer professors of philosophy have ever been philosophers."

During my many ensuing years as a journalist, I continued reading philosophy voraciously on my own. One of my most exhilarating "discoveries" during these years was Walter Kaufmann. Unlike most academic philosophers, Kaufmann was a philosopher who simply happened to make his living by teaching philosophy at a university. Not only did he never lose his childlike love of questioning, he cultivated and nurtured it throughout his life. Kaufmann is best remembered by academics

for his exquisite translations from German into English of many of the books of philosopher Friedrich Nietzsche. But he also wrote a number of seminal philosophical works in which he sculpted his own comprehensive philosophical system dealing with problems central to people's lives. He wrote critically, passionately, Socratically.

In his *The Faith of a Heretic*, Kaufmann wrote this stirring passage:

> Let people who do not know what to do with themselves in this life, but fritter away their time hope for eternal life. If one lives intensely, the time comes when sleep seems bliss. If one loves intensely, the time comes when death seems bliss. . . . The life I want is a life I could not endure in eternity. It is a life of love and intensity, suffering and creation. . . . As one deserves a good night's sleep, one also deserves to die. Why should I hope to wake again? To do what I have not done in the time I've had? All of us have so much more time than we use well. . . . Lives are spoiled and made rotten by the sense that death is distant and irrelevant. . . . [B]ut it makes for a better life if one has a rendezvous with death. . . . There is nothing morbid about thinking and speaking of death. Those who disparage honesty do not know its joys.

The first time I came across this passage, at age thirty, I felt I had unconscionably frittered away much of my life. Kaufmann's words made me realize not how short and precious life is, but

how unbearably long and meaningless much of my life had

seemed to me. And they made me realize how inexcusable it was for me to have allowed my life to take on such soporific dimensions by abandoning my search for meaning. I cannot say that Kaufmann's words jarred me immediately from my lethargy. But it almost brought tears to my eyes to read these words from a modern philosopher, and his words stayed with me. Kaufmann had the uncanny ability to make me ashamed of my slovenly habits of mind and way of life yet at the same time inspire me to make dramatic life changes—even if it took me years to put my ideas into action.

For Kaufmann, philosophy wasn't some pie-in-the-sky discipline. It was personal. It was something to be woven into the fabric of one's being. Kaufmann had immigrated to the United States from Nazi Germany at his parents' behest and had earned his Ph.D. from Harvard at age twenty-four. He had loved ones who were executed or who died in concentration camps. He had seen firsthand in Germany how ordinary citizens' reluctance to question the powers that be—and this, no less, in a society boasting high levels of education and artistic and scientific achievement— had precipitated his homeland's fall into the abyss. For Kaufmann, recapturing the Socratic ethos wasn't some passing fancy; it wasn't some intriguing pet project to while away his professional life. It was a mission of critical import.

I think a thorough reading of Kaufmann's oeuvre shows he believed that civilization might not have a future if it didn't resuscitate its Socratic heritage. Kaufmann helped instill in me the conviction that if humankind was going to stand its ground the next time a madman tried to mislead people with mesmerizing propaganda and dupe them into committing inhumane and irrational acts, then it somehow had to become second nature for the "masses" to seek Socrates.

In the tiny obituary of Kaufmann that appeared in the *New*

York Times the day after he died, little is said about him beyond a mention of his Nietzsche translations—other than that he was known for asking "pesky" questions at meetings of Princeton's philosophy department.

Kaufmann's outspokenness no doubt hindered his career advancement in academic philosophy. He lamented the fact that the pervasive will among modern academic philosophers is the will to pedantry. He called philosophical pedantry "the mode in which the relatively uncreative can be endlessly creative." He took issue with Immanuel Kant and other creative geniuses such as Thomas Aquinas, who is renowned for reconciling Aristotle's philosophy with Christian doctrine to create the orthodox Catholic philosophy, and Georg Wilhelm Friedrich Hegel, a German philosopher whose idealistic system of metaphysics continues to exert a great influence on philosophy. Kaufmann argued that even these great philosophers relied on the crutch of jargon-filled pedantry, "and their genius was diminished by this." Even worse, he noted, "those today who emulate their pedantry do not share their genius." Kaufmann was by no means saying that every philosopher should be doing the same thing. He was not saying that every philosopher need be the "self-appointed critic of the age." But he *was* saying that when every philosopher has abandoned the role of Socratic gadfly, philosophy is in trouble. "It would be a shame if *everybody* waited to criticize until appointed . . . as if one became a gadfly by appointment." Kaufmann saw this as the central problem plaguing academic philosophy. He wrote: "It would be tempting to conclude: what matters is not to revolutionize philosophy, but to make philosophy once again revolutionary."

Employing somewhat milder rhetoric, John Dewey said there was a crying need for a "reconstruction" of philosophy. "In philosophy today there are not many who exhibit confidence about its ability to deal competently with the serious issues of the day," wrote Dewey, who placed great emphasis on the importance of active inquiry in gaining knowledge and who was fond of saying that the subject matter of philosophy is not philosophy but the "problems of men." The prevailing practice among philosophers in his era during the first half of the twentieth century, and even more widespread today, is one of "giving attention to form at the expense of substantial content." Dewey, who railed against philosophers who rendered the subject matter of their studies less rather than more intelligible, called such "withdrawal" by philosophers into the world of pure form "a sign of the extent of the disturbance and unsettlement that now marks" and mars modern life.

Their critiques are echoed by other "glaring exceptions," Socratic spirits within the ranks of academic philosophers. Justus Buchler, a former philosophy professor at Columbia University who specialized in metaphysics, offers this criticism of his peers: "Out of vanity or impatience or unimaginativeness, philosophers prefer censuring one another to finding and articulating the intent in one another's structures. Preoccupation with grammar, innocent enough in itself, has retarded the discovery of meanings, and, in philosophy, has encouraged the confusion of literalness with exactness," he writes in *Nature and Judgment*.

Likewise, in *Portraits from Memory*, Bertrand Russell, an English radical political advocate heralded for his work in logic and the philosophy of mathematics, and winner of the Nobel Prize, devastatingly dismissed such philosophers as involved in "a trivial and uninteresting pursuit. To discuss endlessly what silly people mean when they say silly things may be amusing but can hardly be important. . . ." He said such philosophers remind him of "the shopkeeper of whom I once asked the shortest way to Winchester. He called to a man in the back premises: 'Gentleman wants to know the shortest way to Winchester.' 'Winchester?' an unseen voice replied. 'Aye.' 'Way to Winchester?' 'Aye.' 'Shortest way?' 'Aye.' 'Dunno.' He wanted to get the nature of the question clear, but took no interest in answering it." To Russell, "This is exactly what modern philosophy does for the earnest seeker after

truth. Is it surprising that young people turn to other studies?"

Walter Kaufmann wrote of philosophy's "dual heritage." It is exemplified, on the one hand, by those with existentialist leanings who "have tried to bring philosophy down to earth again like Socrates" and who have "taken up the passionate concern with questions that arise from life, the moral pathos, and the firm belief that, to be serious, philosophy has to be lived." In the other camp are the analytical philosophers, who believe just as fervently that "no moral pathos, no tradition, and no views, however elevated, justify unanalyzed ideas, murky arguments, or a touch of confusion." In every great philosopher, Kaufmann notes, philosophy "occurred in the tension between these two timeless tendencies, now inclining one way, now the other." But "the existentialist and the analytical philosopher are only half of Socrates."

I think Kaufmann overstates the case when he describes a philosopher who primarily has either an existential or analytical bent as "half of Socrates." I think a number of philosophers over the ages have embraced a version of the Socratic method in their own philosophical work. But if philosophers haven't also striven to make their beloved discipline a vibrant and relevant part of the lives of people of all ages and walks of life, then they haven't embraced the Socratic *ethos* for which Socrates gave his life.

Kaufmann anticipated a resurgence of Socratic philosophy, or what I would call the "Socratic tendency." He wrote thirty years ago that "if the feat of Socrates is really to be repeated and philosophy is to have a future outside the academies, there will have to

be philosophers who think in the tension between analysis and existentialism." A number of years ago, when I first read this passage by Kaufmann, I remember thinking: Could I or anyone else pull it off, this feat of bringing Socratic dialogue back to life? If so, where to begin?

Alfred North Whitehead, a British mathematician and philosopher who tried to integrate modern physics into a metaphysics of nature, said famously that the history of philosophy is a mere series of footnotes to Plato. But I'd say that the history of philosophy is all too often a series of misinterpretations and misappropriations and bastardizations of Plato. All too many philosophers in the so-called historical canon, as well as all too many academic philosophers today, have discarded or overlooked the rich and pervasive Socratic bent of Plato's dialogues. They've gerrymandered nuggets here and there from Plato's work, and then recast them to mesh with their own views (which tend to be quasi-mystical at best).

John Herman Randall, Jr., along with his longtime colleague Justus Buchler, is one of the few academics I've encountered who took the Socratic heritage for his own and employed it in wondrous ways. Randall—an interpreter of Greek humanism and Christian ethics, as well as a historian of philosophy and the Western intellectual tradition—maintained that "it was Plato . . . who created the Socrates of the dialogues, and the philosophical tradition" of Socratic inquiry in the process. Randall added that this would seem to imply that Plato "could see all around Socrates, and view him, as we say, objectively." He argued that this feat makes Plato "greater" than Socrates. But I think it is at best an exercise in futility to try to decide which of them is "greater." It is much more worthwhile simply to note that Socrates would have liked nothing better than for his famous pupil to have surpassed him in his command of the method he originated and, through his writing, to pass on to us his legacy.

Randall held that the vast store of visions, both past and present, to which we expose ourselves increases our own store of "imaginative perspectives upon the world."

Christopher
Phillips

Here is not the practice so much as the poetry of ideas. Those visions are perspectives, from differing standpoints, of the activities of men and their ideal enterprises, on the same permanences of man's experience of the world. In seeking the universal structure of that world and of man's varied experience of it and in it, it is an imaginative liberation to look through as many different eyes as we may.

Randall's exhortation to "look through as many eyes as we may" is as good a rationale as any for bringing philosophy "to the people," as Socrates did, in the marketplace. The world of books and scholarship is a world neither Randall nor I could live without. But there are experiences that cannot be had from reading about the experiences of others. Sometimes one has to leap into the proverbial fray and engage the very uncommon "common man" head on, as Socrates did. Buchler and Randall believed that the philosophical life is not just the life of the mind, or of the ivory tower. They took part in philosophical discourse to an unusual degree with the common man. They held public philosophical dialogues on radio and before both lay audiences and professional audiences outside their discipline. Buchler was considered the moral and intellectual leader of Columbia's highly acclaimed general education program in contemporary civilization—a program that dared to blur the artificial boundaries erected between academic disciplines and that strived to reach out to the public. And Randall was at times an activist who put his career on the line to stand up for his beliefs. In 1933 he signed a faculty statement denouncing "rampant economic nationalism and individualism which threaten to sweep the world into another war." Two years later, he and other officers of the American Federation of Teachers resigned in protest against left-wing agitation that they felt was exploiting a labor union by turning it into a political movement to advance their own agenda. In 1940 he led educators to challenge a ban against the appointment of Bertrand Russell to the City College of New York faculty—a ban brought about by Russell's "radical" views on religion and morality. Both he and Buchler were "activist scholars" who aimed to make philosophical inquiry an integral part of the lives of people from many walks of life and to build bridges between the ivory tower and the "real world." After nearly four decades at Columbia, Buchler ended up leaving, apparently at least partly because he no longer felt that the university strongly embraced diverse philosophical thinking. He headed for the State University of New York at Stony Brook, where he founded a graduate program (now defunct) in philosophical perspectives.

Along with those of Walter Kaufmann, the seminal contributions of Buchler and Randall are not to be found in even the most modern dictionaries or encyclopedias of philosophy. Surely their "heretical" approach to philosophizing was one reason why, despite their vital work in their discipline, they came to feel alienated from many of their academic peers—and why they continue to be underappreciated and overlooked.

OUT OF THIS WORLD

I have just entered a diner where Socrates Café is slated to be inaugurated in an insular university town in a remote part of a midwestern state. I try as best I can to hide my shock over the standing-room-only crowd crammed into the place. All of the swivel stools along the long counter are filled, as well as all the rows of folding chairs that have been set up in a semicircle in the dining section facing the counter. And people are still streaming in.

I'd been invited by a philosophy professor to initiate a Socrates Café. The professor, who had once been a student of Justus Buchler's and decided to earn his doctorate in philosophy with Buchler's encouragement, told me in a moving letter he'd written me that after teaching philosophy for forty years he had "become a bit jaded." He said he had entered the field "with the idealistic hope that philosophy could make some difference in the world and influence the development of our culture." It seemed clear that he had also entered philosophy, as I had, seeking Socrates, but that he had not found this "dangerous corrupter of the youth," as he described him, to reside within the world of academia. "No philosopher of my acquaintance," he wrote me, "has been brought to trial in this country to my knowledge for any reason whatsoever," much less for the charge leveled against Socrates of corrupting youth by teaching them to think critically. The professor said this was "evidence that academic philosophy (at least) is either totally ignored or fits in so well with the received capitalistic worldview as to be almost invisible."

He said the mental effort he devoted to "trying to figure out what difference my teaching has made in the world" is "a discouraging occupation." Making his career seem even less redeeming is the fact that, as he noted in his letter, academic philosophers are not much appreciated anymore, even by their peers in academia. His own fear, he said, is that most of the big state and public colleges and universities will do away altogether with philosophy departments. "I know my own school," he wrote, "is headed in that direction and that our department is under fire from an administration that would like to do away with our whole department, since Socrates didn't have to take up valuable space in a building on campus."

Here was one professor who saw hope for philosophy—outside of academia, where Socratic discourse, if nurtured properly, stood a chance of flourishing. "Your idea of philosophy cafés is a good one and may catch on," he said to me at the end of his letter.

I wrote him back and mentioned in an offhand way that perhaps sometime I could help him get a Socrates Café started in his neck of the woods. I was more than a little surprised when he contacted me shortly thereafter to tell me that he would be willing to make arrangements to find a diner or coffeehouse in town to host the gathering if I'd come up to inaugurate it.

I accepted at once.

Two months later, here I am in his hometown, at a newly opened café situated close to the campus where the professor teaches. Among the Socrates Café participants is virtually the entire contingent of professors—six in all, I believe—from the philosophy department at the nearby university. My host had said that in its heyday the department had upwards of twenty to twenty-five philosophy professors. With one exception, the professors are middle-aged, and most are considerably beyond middle age. Before the discussion gets under way, one of them laments to me that every time a philosophy professor retires, the university administration refuses to hire a new one, furthering the department's decline.

As usual, at the outset of this Socrates Café I ask for a question to discuss. A pile of textbooks in her lap, a pen and notepad in hand, a college student asks, "Is there only a subjective world or is there such a thing as a world of ultimate reality?"

How, I wonder, can we do justice to this question? How can

we throw our arms around it in just a couple of hours?

Philosophers have struggled with what precisely a world is since the dawn of their discipline. For instance, Thomas Hobbes wrote in *Leviathan* that "the world" is "the whole mass of all things that are." But he never makes it quite clear what he means by "all things." Immanuel Kant is among the ranks of philosophers who believe in two worlds. In his "two worlds" philosophy, Kant distinguished between the *phenomenal* world, which is knowable by the senses and interpreted by the mind, and the *noumenal* world, which lies behind the world of space and time and cause and effect, and is unknowable. In counterpoint, Ludwig Wittgenstein declared in *Tractatus Logico-Philosophicus* that it is "nonsense" to speak of an unknowable world. To Wittgenstein, the world is "the totality of facts," which contain a logical structure that shape and delimit our world. While facts are inherently knowable, Wittgenstein said "we must be silent" about the so-called unknowable, because we shouldn't speak about things we can't and don't know.

"What is a world?" I wonder out loud, almost more to myself than to the rest of the group. "What is a world?"

A woman in a loud sweat suit who has just taken her seat as I ask this replies, "I think that cliché 'The world is what you make of it' has a lot of truth to it. If there are Catholics, atheists, Hindus, Platonists, skeptics, New Agers, seekers, pagans, occultists, and the lot here in this room, then we all are in a sense in a world of our own. A Christian would think with conviction that this world was only a stepping stone to an otherworldly existence. He imagines 'God' is with him at every moment. Others might also have convictions of otherworldly things, whether in the here and now or in the hereafter. But if I have no such belief, then my world here and now, my entire disposition to whatever world we

170

have in common, would be in many respects violently different from theirs."

One young man with a shaved head and an expression of affected indifference says smugly, "There is no such thing as a world, only worlds. We all live in our own worlds. We're all islands."

"We seem to be communicating with one another right now," I point out to him. "This would seem to indicate that to some degree we share worlds."

"Communication is meaningless," he replies with a deadpan look. "We never understand each other."

"So," I say to him, "you and I are not communicating, not understanding each other, right now? What we're saying to one another is just gibberish?"

He just stares at me. He doesn't so much as nod in agreement or shake his head in dissent. He just stares. Soon he gets up and retreats from our immediate world.

One of the professors then says, "Isn't there a world with a view from nowhere? I think Aristotle showed pretty convincingly that such a world exists."

The student who posed the question seems to have come prepared to take this issue on. "Aristotle is not at all supporting a view from nowhere," she says firmly. "All he was saying is that whenever we speak of such a view, we are speaking of it *in relation to* ourselves." She pauses to collect her thoughts. "Aristotle *did* think there's such a thing as nowhere—namely, the universe as a whole—but he did *not* think that there is such a thing as a view from nowhere."

I see out of the corner of my eye that the "Aristotelian" professor is looking at her with something resembling a mixture of envy and awe and animosity.

Another student taking part in the dialogue soon says, "If this view from nowhere is a view offered by a human being, it isn't a view from nowhere at all. This is really a view that is from somewhere."

An elegantly dressed middle-aged woman with delicate features abruptly stands up and says, "The only way to know if there's a view from nowhere is to answer this question: If a tree falls to the ground and no one is there to hear it, does it still make a sound?" She sits down, looking quite pleased with herself.

One student, an earnest physics major, responds, "Whether a tree that falls out of earshot of humankind makes a sound has no relevancy at all. It's a moot point. It wouldn't even be a question if there weren't someone on hand in some way at some point in time to acknowledge that the event occurred or might've occurred."

"Someone, at some point, must 'know,' or 'speculate' from evidence, that a tree fell to the ground," he continues. "If someone concludes the tree in question fell to the ground, he might then also reasonably speculate that it must have made a sound when it hit the ground. And he can only make such a speculation in this instance if, on another occasion, he has actually seen a tree fall to the ground and make a sound on impact, or if he knows of solid evidence that says that trees that fall to the ground always or almost always make a sound. The alleged fallen tree, and the resulting sound, has to be verified and validated somehow. One way to do it is to reconstruct what took place when it fell, to speculate on what transpired by extrapolating from 'real' cases, from 'real' evidence, that we are familiar with and that are similar to or identical with this one. And in order to speculate plausibly like this, much less to draw sound conclusions, you have to have a fund of knowledge to draw on."

I look to the woman who'd posed the question about the tree to see if she wants to respond, and she shakes her head no.

Another professor then charges that some participants are in effect offering a relativist viewpoint. "Some," he says, "seem to be hinting that there is no such thing as universals. But mathematical symbols are the quintessential proof that there are universals, and so they epitomize the view from nowhere."

"But," I say, "don't these so-called universals only exist in relation to the human beings who pondered them, who invented them, 'imagined' them into existence? And if this is the case, isn't 'nowhere' really 'somewhere' quite specific, namely our minds, our selves?"

He won't hear of it. "You just don't want to accept that there are universals that exist independent of humans," he says dismissively.

Then another professor tries telling a joke. Interrupting a student who is just starting to say something, he says with a sardonic smile, "If a professor fell to the ground, would anyone hear him?" No one even snickers.

The students, though, are mustering the confidence and courage to challenge me and their professors. One student says he's just read a novel, *The Manticore*, by Robertson Davies. "Davies spoke about 'the view from elsewhere' in his book," he says. "Maybe that's the best we can do, seek to embrace views from elsewhere, views besides our own. Maybe this is the way to go about expanding our own worldview. A view from nowhere, on the other hand, seems to me to take us, well, nowhere. It's a fun notion to play with, but in the end, it's a nowhere view."

"But isn't a view from nowhere, being a particular view offered here by particular people, one of the views from elsewhere?" I ask him. "In that sense, isn't this view well worth considering and examining as exhaustively as possible, even if some of you come to conclude that it isn't one you can agree with?

"What's more," I say, "isn't the view from nowhere really a

view of 'ultimate objectivity,' a view that we can never attain but that we can strive to move closer and closer toward?"

The student doesn't answer. He is mulling this over, and he doesn't have any immediate response. A couple of professors seem heartened that I appear now to be "defending" their beloved view from nowhere. I even overhear one murmur "Exactly" following my response. But in keeping with the Socratic method, I am not offering a defense of any view in particular so much as I am insisting that we examine every view from as many angles and vantage points as possible, insisting that we consider compelling objections and alternatives.

Christopher Phillips

Eventually, I begin soliciting responses from the "silent participants" who are always in attendance at each Socrates Café. They listen intently to the discussion but either don't feel compelled to speak or don't feel comfortable doing so unless called upon. When I ask them if they want to say something, almost invariably they have penetrating comments to share. One student sitting at the counter with me says, "To me a world has to be something I can see and feel and touch physically. This view from nowhere has no meaning to me. I've been trying to consider it seriously, but it just seems empty, meaningless. You may say that it can be seen as a view toward more and more objectivity, but I don't think that's the way he meant it." He nods in the direction of the professor. "I think he sees it like a view from heaven, like a God's-eye view."

Then a diffident woman sitting at the far end of the counter, who somehow seems both bothered and delighted that I've asked her to speak, says after a considerable pause, "I think that the person who said near the beginning of our dialogue that there are only worlds, not a world, was more or less right. I think we are all islands, in a sense. For instance, a student of poetry, a student of game theory, a student of atomic physics, a student of cultural anthropology: each studies his island of knowledge and has very little concern for the islands of knowledge that concern the others. They're all convinced that their islands are the most worthwhile. And they don't understand one another's islands very well, if at all.

"But as John Donne wrote, 'No man is an island'—not really. People and their areas of knowledge are not islands unto themselves, even if they like to think they are. Their islands constantly intersect and overlap. Because they're each inquiring, in their own way, into what makes this world the way it is, and into why the world is the way it is. So theirs is a common pursuit, no matter how different their pursuits seem on the face of it."

We listen intently as she continues, no longer reluctant to speak. "Sure, they may pursue their studies in isolation. But all that means is that each has devoted herself to one of the countless perspectives that our world contains. And the fact is that each in her own way is also seeking to *unify* her world through her specialized field of study. Whether it's a physicist or a poet or an anthropologist or an economist or a theologian, each uses the language and myths of her field to try to create a big picture, a unified vision, of the world."

"I thoroughly agree with her," chimes in a professor from the university's department of religion. He is the only professor in attendance who is not clustered with the group of academic philosophers, and until now he has had a quizzical, almost bemused look on his face.

"And what does her view of the world say about the world that we live in?" I ask him.

"It says that our world is one that inspires us to see it whole," he replies. "The many ways and means we go about trying to pres-

Christopher Phillips

ent a unified vision of the world just shows how multifaceted the world is. Just like William James said long ago, our world is without question a pluralistic one." In his books *The Varieties of Religious Experience* and *A Pluralistic Universe,* James asserted that it would be intellectually dishonest and simplistic to try to reduce, one to the other, the vast array of individual, cultural, and religious approaches and perspectives to which people subscribe. Rather, to James, all of the "actual peculiarities of the world" show irrefutably that our world is open, pluralistic, and ever evolving.

"And what she said so eloquently," the professor goes on to say, "is in complete agreement with both James and Etienne Gilson, the French Catholic philosopher and so-called radical theologian, who like James says that our world is boundlessly new and creative and allows for endless exploration from countless perspectives."

"And what I think this means," says another student who until now has not said a word, "is that there are not only many different styles and ways of thinking about the world, but that there are different forms of intelligence—religious, philosophical, scientific, poetic, you name it."

In his renowned theory of multiple intelligences, Howard Gardner, a professor of education and psychology at Harvard, identified seven distinct types of intelligence: linguistic, logical-mathematical, bodily-kinesthetic, spatial, musical, interpersonal, and intrapersonal. But as provocative and groundbreaking as this theory is widely deemed, I don't think he has identified *types* of intelligence at all; rather, he has pinpointed some of the *ways* in which intelligence—philosophical, aesthetic, scientific, intuitive, what have you—can be expressed.

Another participant then says, "Building on what a number of people here have said, I think that our world is one that contains within it an infinite number of worlds, one for each person, because we all have perspectives on the world that are at least slightly different."

Gottfried Wilhelm Leibniz, an eminent rationalist philosopher who, along with Sir Isaac Newton, was an inventor of calculus and a forefather of modern mathematical logic, maintained that there are an infinite number of possible worlds, all of which God considered before creating the actual world, which is "the best of the possible worlds." Leibniz believed that reason dictated that everything occurring within our world ultimately is good, because God had to have created a universe better than any other that could possibly have been created. He explained away evil by maintaining that its existence in this world has to be an integral part of the perfection of the whole world. The French philosopher, essayist, novelist, and social critic Voltaire, who did not think evil in this world could be so easily explained away, lampooned Leibniz via the character Dr. Pangloss in his classic satire *Candide*. Ridiculing the Panglossian perspective that "all is for the best in the best of all possible worlds," no matter how evil an action or occurrence, Voltaire believed that we must take concrete action to combat and thwart the evil in this world. "We must cultivate our garden," he wrote.

One after another, the silent participants chime in. The views are becoming richly diverse as more and more participants become comfortable and confident contributing to the dialogue. It is clear who the bold thinkers are, and who are not.

Then, to my dismay, long before the discussion is scheduled to end, one of the professors stands up and says, "Let's call it a night. Thanks for coming." Just as the discussion is beginning to take on a momentum of its own, it is abruptly terminated. No one has asked us if we want to end it now. But the professor's reflex seems to say: "Class dismissed."

UNEXPECTED QUESTIONS

Christopher
Phillips

In many ways, we barely scratched the surface of the rich question we were delving into. We had yet to distinguish between objective and subjective reality, much less take a stab at delineating "ultimate reality" (much less "reality" itself!). And we had not begun to pin down criteria for all the different types of worlds that may or may not exist. Yet I wasn't overly discouraged by this dialogue's peremptory end. Because I knew there would be occasions at future Socrates Cafés to tackle variations of these questions about differing worlds and realities. Just as I knew that such a discussion could be prompted by the most unexpected questions.

EMBRACING THE "WHAT WITHIN"

"Why is what?"

I am facilitating a Socrates Café at a cavernous bookstore-café overlooking the coast of northern California. I ask for possible questions to discuss and this is what one person has pitched to me. Many of the thirty or so participants give him a rather queer look. I think that I must have been looking at him a bit oddly myself.

I want to know. I *have* to know. I pick that question. And then I ask him, "What the hell do you mean?"

"I'm an engineering student," he says in a pronounced Russian accent. He has a genteel manner and looks to be in his early twenties, though he is almost completely bald. He goes on to say, "I often study a variety of 'whats'—subatomic particles, electromagnetic fields, polymers, bridges, what have you. And I often ask myself why these 'whats' exist or why they are capable of existing. It has occurred to me that there would be no 'why' without there first being a 'what.'"

He draws a breath. "So," he says, "why is what?"

One woman seems a bit nonplussed. "This is just mental masturbation," she says.

"Why?" I ask her.

"Because it doesn't make sense," she says. "I think that he's just playing with words. Philosophically, I don't think it's possible to talk about it."

"But he just explained what he meant," I say. "He even went so far as to explain what he meant by 'what.' He's already answered 'What is what?' from his perspective and now he wants us to help him answer 'Why is what?'"

"I think he was just thinking fast," she says. "I don't think he really had any idea what he was asking."

Raul, a regular Socrates Café-goer who until now has been open to and enthusiastic about every question we've ever discussed, sides with this woman. "You can't ask why is what," he says flatly.

"You can't even ask the question?" I say. "That sounds rather . . . dictatorial. Who are any of us to say that this question can't so much as be asked?"

Not ready to give in, he says, "I'm sure that *Socrates* would never have discussed a question like 'Why is what?'"

This rouses additional people to the engineering student's defense. "Well, Socrates couldn't discuss *everything*," says a man whose sideburns and hairstyle match those on the portrait of Elvis emblazoned on his T-shirt. "Besides that, I don't think Socrates would've dismissed any question that any person wanted to honestly engage in with him. Not only would Socrates have asked 'Why is what?' I think he would've asked, 'What is what?' 'Are humans "whats"?' 'Is everything that exists, materially or spiritually, some type of "what"?'"

"He's right," says the woman beside Raul, a friend of his who always accompanies him to these gatherings but rarely says a word. "Let's look at this young man's question," she says to her friend. "Let's explore it, and let's try to keep our prejudices about it on the back burner for a while."

"Why is what . . . why is what . . ." he mutters to himself, grudgingly.

Then my wife Cecilia, nodding in the direction of the engineering student, says, "When he first asked this question, I didn't think it made any sense either. But in my native language, 'Why is what?' is *¿Porqué es qué?* And I realize that the first word in the question—*porqué*—includes in it the second question word, *qué*. So, in Spanish, when we ask for a reason—when we ask 'Why?'—we are asking at the same time for the subject of our question, namely 'What?' So at the same time I'm asking for a reason I am also asking for the thing itself. In my native language, why and what are inseparable."

One man who has been recalcitrant about discussing the question looks at Cecilia with a somewhat bemused look on his face. Finally he says, "You've just changed my point of view 180 degrees. I couldn't let my imagination break through the language barrier and liberate itself to inquire into the question." He looks a bit sheepish while admitting this, but he also looks exhilarated.

The engineering student says to him, "I'm glad you raised the objection to my question. Because I've been wondering if I really knew what it was I was trying to ask. It seems to me that by questioning my question, we've come up with answers we never would have discovered if we'd just tried to answer it outright."

Then, before laughing sheepishly, he says, "I'm finally ready to embrace 'the what within.'"

"Well," I say to the group, "Before we embrace it too tightly, let's try to examine more carefully what, if anything, this 'what' is or can be." Directing my gaze to the engineering student, I say, "You equate 'whats' with subatomic particles, electromagnetic fields, polymers, bridges. So I gather you're saying that in order for something to qualify as a 'what,' it has to be a material substance."

He nods with satisfaction and says, "Exactly. Everything that exists is a material substance made up of fundamental particles."

While legions of philosophers and scientists would agree with him, none other than Aristotle, Plato's student and Alexander the Great's tutor, rejected the dogma of fundamental particles, finding it more akin to wishful thinking than a provable hypothesis. In his *Physics*, Aristotle said substance is "first for us, within which we distinguish principles, causes, and elements." Substance is not just matter, according to Aristotle; rather, substance is the source for everything, spiritual as well as material, tangible as well as intangible. He is also indicating that substance cannot be understood or known apart from its qualities, powers, and manifestations, and so cannot be reduced to irreducible simples.

Despite the fact that he and Plato were the most influential philosophers of the Western tradition, most everyone who came after Aristotle ignored his views on this subject apparently because they found them so outlandish. But the eighteenth-century British empiricist philosopher David Hume, famous for his arguments against the proofs for God's existence, was one of the few who used Aristotle's rich line of thinking as a springboard to his own conceptualization of substance. Hume wrote in *A Treatise of Human Nature* that "we have no idea of external substance, distinct from the ideas of particular qualities." He said this must mean that we also have no notion of the mind, "distinct from the particular perceptions" the mind has of particular objects. Hume took these two "givens" to set forth the principle that nature has many dimensions—physical, social, psychological, and aesthetic dimensions, among others—and that each is "essential" and "fundamental" in its own right in the grand scheme of things. None of these dimensions exists in isolation; they overlap and coalesce and mutually influence one another at every turn.

While Aristotle, embracing the prevailing cosmology of his day, held that certain substances, like "the heavenly bodies," were immutable and therefore "complete," he nonetheless was in agreement with Hume that there is nothing simple about any type of substance. According to this philosophical perspective, a substance, or a "what," is every bit as much a substance because of what it does, what it can do, what it might do, what might be done to it, as it is a substance because of what it's made of. Its actualities, its forces, its powers, its potential, its history: all are part and parcel of its "ultimate" or "fundamental" makeup. Hume believed that all of these facets of substance are equally essential, ultimate, fundamental. To isolate any one of them not only would make substance so much less than what it really is but would distort substance beyond repair.

"Can good be a 'what'?" I ask the engineer.

His satisfied look disappears. "What?" he asks.

"Can good be a 'what'? If, for instance, I eat a hamburger, and I say, 'It tastes good,' is my description of the hamburger as 'good' a what? Or if I rescue someone from possibly drowning and my deed is described as a 'good deed,' is this good a what?"

The engineer looks baffled. Raul comes to his aid. "The deed itself is a what," he says. "Just as the hamburger itself is a what. But the good isn't a what. The good is just a quality of the material substance."

"Just a quality?" I say. "Isn't a quality a what? Isn't the quality of the hamburger or the quality of the deed of rescuing a person who is drowning also a what?"

The woman who earlier characterized this discussion as mental masturbation says, "It is indeed a what." Looking at the engineer, she says, "You're a materialist. But things that aren't material are whats too. A quality is every bit as much of a what as anything else under the sun. Everything that exists is a what. In fact, qualities are what make whats whats. All whats have qualities, all qualities have whats."

She pauses to collect her thoughts and then says, "If I look at you and say, 'You're handsome,' then I'm saying that handsome is a what every bit as much as I'm saying that you are a what. If the quality handsome were not a what, then I wouldn't be able to use it. Handsome is a word that describes you. A word is an entity, a what, used for a specific purpose, to communicate. So these words that we share, words like good or handsome, are also whats. I'm an English teacher and I teach people to work with words. Every single word they work with are whats. Words are manipulated to form things, to build works of literature or letters or what have you, just like chemicals are used to construct certain things."

"Aren't words also what enable us to speak about, and to identify, whats?" I ask.

She looks at me quizzically.

"What you're saying, I think," the engineer says, looking at me, "is that words are what we use to point to or point out or describe in some way the real substances that the universe is made of. But I still don't think that words are the same as whats. Whats are reality, whats are what the universe is made of. And words are among our tools to make sense of the whats that make up reality."

Before anyone can get a word in edgewise, he sighs and says, "But I guess words are whats too. Otherwise we couldn't speak about or describe what words are or what they do."

He turns toward the English teacher and says, "You seem to think that words and qualities aren't material. And I realize now that where I went wrong was when I said that only concrete things like hamburgers and polymers are real or material. But words are real, words are material, too. If a word appears on a piece of paper, it can only do so because it is made of something, just as the piece of paper it appears on is a something, a what. And if the word appears in your mind as a thought, it can only do so because your mind is made of a concrete substance, your brain." He pauses for a considerable while. Then he says, again focusing his gaze on the teacher, "What I think I'm trying to articulate is that you seem to distinguish between material and immaterial things, and you seem to be saying that they're two altogether different kinds of whats. And what I'm saying now is that there is no such thing as an immaterial thing, that all these things are material, even though they appear to be very different sorts of material things."

Christopher Phillips

"So words are the whats, our articulated thoughts, that we use to point to the whats 'out there' in reality?" I ask.

"Something like that," he says. His views are strikingly similar to those of F. H. Bradley, the foremost British idealist philosopher, who in his seminal work *Appearance and Reality* speaks of reality as a union of a "what" and a "that," in which our thoughts—the whats—give the form or universal to the substance or matter of reality, the "that."

There is a loud laugh that jolts our collective attention. It comes from Raul. Looking at the engineer, he says, "What threw me when you first posed this question was the way you asked the question. You asked it in a way that I couldn't grasp. I think the way a child would ask this question is, 'Why is there something rather than nothing?' or 'Why is there a what?'"

"According to Heidegger, man is the only being who questions Being itself, who questions why there is something rather than nothing," I say. "We seem to be proof that he's right."

"Being!" Raul says in a voice so loud that it startles us. "Now there's a word." Again directing his gaze at the engineer, he asks,

"Is *what* everything that is? Is *what*, in other words, that which has being?"

This time the engineer's response comes quickly. "Yes, absolutely."

"I disagree," says Cecilia. "What about things that don't yet exist, things that a philosopher might say are in a 'state of becoming'? They're whats too."

"I'm afraid I don't follow you," the engineer says. Judging from the looks of some of the others, he speaks for them as well.

"Well, I'm a potential senior citizen," she says. "If I live long enough, I eventually will *be* a senior citizen. And what I'm saying is, this potential within me, this person that I have the potential to become, but haven't yet become, is just as much a what as who I am at this very moment."

An elderly woman with large, animated eyes says to Cecilia, "I'm the senior citizen that you potentially are." Then, turning her attention to the rest of us, she says in Latin, "*Sum quod eris, quod es, ante fui, pro me, pregor, ora!*—I am what you will become, what you are I have already been, please pray for my soul."

"That's beautiful, but I'm afraid I just don't agree," the engineer says. "I don't think potential is a what. Until the potential is realized, it's . . . nothing."

"But once the potential is realized, you also realize that it was there within you all along," Cecilia says. "When I was a child, I always dreamed of being a dancer. Then, when I was a teenager, I began taking dance classes with the Martha Graham School of Contemporary Dance. I've been dancing ever since. I *am* a dancer. I'm many other things too, and I have the potential to become many other things. And I don't agree with you that being a potential dancer—that having the potential to be a dancer—is nothing until I actually become a dancer. Becoming is just as much a what as being is."

"I see what you're saying," the English teacher chimes in. "For instance, an acorn is a potential oak tree. Experience shows that if it is properly cultivated, that's what it will become." Nodding at the engineer, she continues, "Now, you might say that all it is is an acorn, and we can say nothing more about it until it becomes something else. But even if it never actually becomes an oak tree, we can still say that, under optimal conditions, it has the potential to become one. And I would agree with Cecilia that that potential is also a what."

"So change is a what?" I ask her.

"Yes indeed," she says. "Change is a process, and that process is a what."

"So . . . change is a real process, and that which is real is a what," I then say.

She hesitates just a moment before saying, "Yes. Exactly."

"But an acorn, under optimal circumstances, has no choice but to become an oak tree," I say. "Just as Cecilia, under optimal circumstances, will eventually become a senior citizen. These are things that apparently can't be controlled or manipulated—at least, not yet. But even though she may have had the potential to become a dancer, she could just as easily have opted never to realize that potential."

"Either way, the potential was there," says the English teacher. "Some types of potential are innate, or they're instinctive, and are beyond our or anyone else's control. But some types, at least where human beings are concerned, entail choice."

"And either way, the potential is real?" I ask.

"Yes, absolutely," she says. "It's real whether or not I ever discover it or tap into it. And of course there's many areas of potential I would never ever want to tap into. For instance, I, like everyone, have the potential to do harm to others, but because of my value system, it's a potential I'd never want to realize."

There is a pleasant lull in the conversation.

I finally ask, "Is a unicorn a what?"

"Yes, and no," says a man who arrived late to the conversation. "It doesn't exist like a real animal such as a horse or a giraffe exists. But it exists in your imagination, it exists in paintings, it exists in some books. It's an imaginary what."

"This is where I don't agree," the engineer says. "I agree that imagination is real, because imagination is part of the mind of a real human being. And I agree that the painting of a unicorn is real, and that a book about a unicorn is real, because paintings and books are real; they're whats. But the unicorn in and of itself is not real. It's not a what. Because there's no such thing as a real unicorn." He smiles and adds, "At least, I don't think there is." Not for the first time, he sighs deeply and then says, "But now I'm questioning all my assumptions about what's a real what and what isn't."

His now-broad smile seems at odds with his deeply furrowed brow. He eventually says, "I'm starting to wonder if I have any idea what's what."

WHAT'S WHAT?

He's not alone. This was an issue that perplexed Socrates a great deal. One of Plato's Socratic dialogues, *Phaedo*, centers on the cause of "coming-to-be" and "ceasing-to-be" of substances, or whats, and what those whats are made of. Indeed, since long before Socrates, philosophers and nonphilosophers alike have been engaged in a quest to find the Holy Grail of Substances—the Ultimate What, the Simplest of Simples—that can't be reduced or broken down even further.

In fact, many cosmologists now claim at long last to have peered beneath all known qualities and to have discovered substance itself in its pure, unadulterated, irreducible form. They call that substance . . . string. One-dimensional, vibrating, looped strands. And they claim that combinations of these vibrating strings can account for every single thing at the most microscopic level—a discovery, they say, that unifies all theories of the physical world by bridging what had seemed to be the unbridgeable chasm between general relativity and quantum mechanics.

Christopher Phillips

Brian Greene, a physicist at Columbia University, is an ardent advocate of "string theory," the theory of the Ultimate Simple Substance. In *The Elegant Universe*, he writes that "[f]rom one principle—that everything at its most microscopic level consists of combinations of strands—string theory provides a single explanatory framework capable of encompassing all forces and all matter." Greene and most of his fellow cosmologists believe everything observed can be reduced to these tiny one-dimensional loops, which they claim provide "a framework with the capacity to explain every fundamental feature upon which the universe is constructed." Greene believes string theory holds promise as "an unshakable pillar of coherence, forever assuring us that the universe is a comprehensible place." He lauds its potential as "the deepest possible theory of physics," or "T.O.E. [theory of everything]—the ultimate explanation of the universe at its most microscopic level."

But is this latest attempt to pin down an Ultimate What really the "conceptual leap" Greene claims it to be? Is it really a "landmark turning point" that has "given us well-founded hope that we are on the right and possibly final track" toward unifying all scientific knowledge? Or is it really nothing new at all, perhaps representing little more than pouring old conceptual wine into new skins? The sixth century B.C. reductionist pre-Socratic philosophers Democritus and Leucippus believed the universe was made up of fundamental particles moving in empty space. And after them, René Descartes, Isaac Newton, Leibniz, and John Locke all maintained that the simplest of substances was "fundamental," "ultimate," "absolute".

By contrast, the Columbia philosopher Justus Buchler believed there are no such things as simples. Rather, according to Buchler, everything is a complex—not complex, but *a* complex. "Whatever is," Buchler says in his *Metaphysics of Natural Complexes*, "is a natural complex." Nothing, he says, is "more 'real,' more 'natural,' more 'genuine,' or more 'ultimate' than any other." Anything that we've conceptualized and articulated and limned in some way—whether it's considered primarily a product of the human imagination or a substantive physical object—is a natural complex in its singular fashion and has equal standing with all other natural complexes. Whether speaking of a quark, a void, or a unicorn, of antimatter, a fire-breathing dragon, or a symphony, Buchler says you are speaking of a natural complex, each of which has its unique integrity, its own defining and distinguishing functions and properties and powers, which make it in some way and to some degree distinct from everything else. Buchler's term "natural complex" is intended to replace the murky concepts of "thing" or "entity," which are typically associated only with "material" substance. While Buchler thinks that no natural complex is more or less real than any other, I think he would be on firmer footing if he had taken the time to note that there are different types of "real"—such as substantively real, imaginatively real, spiritually real, morally real, ineffably real. And all these types are themselves natural complexes that in some manner inform and describe and interrelate with one another.

When Buchler says everything is a natural complex, he

means everything: "Relations, structures, processes, societies, human individuals, human products, physical bodies, words and bodies of discourse, ideas, qualities, contradictions, meanings, possibilities, myths, laws, duties, feelings, illusions, reasonings, dreams—all are natural complexes." This does not mean that all natural complexes are of equal use or value in discriminating and discovering the physical universe. But it does mean in all instances that there's no such thing as an irreducible simple—that every natural complex over and under and through the sun is composed of a variety of distinguishing and dynamic characteristics and functions. By this principle, upon close inspection, even the submicroscopic string, the so-called Ultimate Substance of the string theory cosmologists, is an intricate complex of singular yet intertwining traits and properties and powers that give it a unique integrity that is no more simple and irreducible than the natural complex we call the universe.

Christopher
Phillips

Lee Smolin, a cosmologist of Pennsylvania State University, argues, in opposition to the string theorists, that the universe in which we live, far from being composed of fixed and immutable simples, has "so much *variety* that no two observers experience the same thing, and no moment ever repeats itself." Buchler would agree with Smolin that "the old search for the absolute," the old belief in a "final destination," is "heavy" and has "weighed us down long enough."

Buchler's novel approach to metaphysics seems to herald what Smolin calls "the lightness of the new search for knowledge." This search, he says, is based on an underlying philosophy that asserts that "the universe is a network of relations; that what was once thought to be absolute is always subject to evolution and renegotiation; that the complete truth about the world is not graspable as any single point of view, but only resides in the totality of several or many distinct views"; and this accounts for the fact that the universe has "the perpetual birth of novelty."

You may well differ with the perspective of Smolin or Buchler, or that of Greene. But by entertaining radically different perspectives on what makes this universe the way it is, you might now be better able to tackle in a more fruitful way such questions as: What is simple? What is absolute? What is fundamental? What type of theory of the universe can best unify all the evidence we have on hand? What type of theory can best help us envisage new possibilities and probabilities of what the universe is and might become—including who we are and might become? What type of universe is really more elegant—one of irreducible simples, or one of ever-changing complexes?

INQUIRING MINDS WANT TO KNOW

Even if science succeeded in unifying its field theory, would this really serve as the ultimate foundation, as the "final resting place," for unifying all knowledge?

It is often overlooked that are there many types of scientific knowledge. And there are many types of knowledge besides scientific knowledge, just as there are many legitimate and fruitful types of inquiry besides scientific inquiry. There is religious inquiry, psychological inquiry, aesthetic inquiry, humanistic inquiry, and philosophical inquiry, among many others—and there are no tidy divides between these realms of exploration. What's more, there is no such thing as *the* scientific method of inquiry. Rather, there are many versions and types of scientific inquiry, just as there are of all other forms of inquiry.

Recognizing this, John Herman Randall, Jr., asks, "Is there a common enterprise of inquiry to which all our arts and sciences and humanities contribute? Have we found it?" His own answer is: "In asking our question, for a coherent and adequate view of the world, whatever our special knowledges, we are all in the end humanists and philosophers."

Christopher Phillips

I'm not at all sure that "we are all humanists and philosophers" merely because each of us may attempt to seek a "coherent and adequate" view of the world. A madman seeking power might manipulate questions in order to promote a "coherent and adequate" view of the world that demands the annihilation of people of certain races or ethnicities. A doomsday guru might ask only questions leading to answers that gibe with his "adequate and coherent" eschatological philosophy, so he can persuade his followers to commit mass suicide. Such people are not philosophers and humanists.

Clearly, many types of worldviews might seem to their proponents "adequate and coherent"—but such views might also be nonredemptive at best, inhumane at worst.

What type of worldview should we strive for?

The French novelist, critic, and essayist André Gide noted that the worth of any type of worldview is not only its adequacy and coherency "but also, and above all . . . the impetus it gives to the mind to make fresh discoveries and new proofs . . . the new vistas it opens, and the barriers it breaks down . . . the weapons it forges." Inhumane and intolerant worldviews do not allow for such ends.

V

Why Ask Why?

?

—ANONYMOUS

?

Christopher
Phillips

For a long time, the question has suffered at our hands. It isn't just that many of us fear questions. Rather, many of us seem to have only the flimsiest idea of the question's power and potential. And many of us no longer seem to have the faintest idea how to use it.

Consider: Is the glass half empty or half full?

There's something wrong with this question. It seems to allow only two possible answers. The problem with this question as set forth is a mirror of the problem with society at large. All too often we're indoctrinated to think in terms of "either-or." Is that man good or is he evil? Is that child gifted or isn't she? It never occurs to many of us that a child can be gifted in many ways, and not so in many others, that a man can be good in many ways, and yet evil in others.

We need to start asking: Is this really the best way to ask this question? Or are there other ways, ways that might lead to more fruitful answers?

We need a new generation of philosophers to transform all the old questions. By doing so, they will, as the English philosopher and classicist Gilbert Ryle put it, "give mankind a different air to breathe."

At one gathering of the Philosophers Club at Cesar Chavez Elementary School in San Francisco, I asked my fellow gang members for ideas for a question to discuss. They came up with a bunch of promising candidates: Can a lie ever be good? What is age? What is tolerance? These kids love to come up with questions.

Then Rafi said, "We could just keep going around in circles and asking question after question. We'd learn a lot just by doing that." He was right.

Then Jennifer asked, "What *is* a question?"

What a question! This was philosophical pay dirt.

"A question is something you try to answer," fellow club member Pilar replied.

"Why do we ask questions in the first place?" I asked.

"Because we wonder," Wilson said.

"Because we want to gain knowledge," said Arturo.

"Because we're curious," said Maria.

"Because we've observed something we don't understand," Eduardo said.

"What would life be without questions?" I asked.

"Boring," said Estefania.

"Nothing," said Jennifer.

"Impossible," said Rafi.

Rosa looked perplexed by these answers. "What do you think of what they said?" I asked her.

"Well, they may be right," she said, though her face indicated she felt otherwise. Then she said, "But what about that saying 'Curiosity killed the cat'?"

"Is it possible to be too curious?" I ask out loud.

TOO CURIOUS?

As I wait for responses, I wonder, to myself, whether under certain circumstances it just might be possible to be too curious, as much as I want to think otherwise. For ages thinkers have dealt with the question of whether we are too curious—whether it would be wise, or at least prudent, to put limits on how much we should aspire to know. Contemporary essayist and literary critic George Steiner, in *In Bluebeard's Castle*, says our civilization may be "marked by a readiness not to endure rather than curtail the risks of thought." Although Steiner suspects that the boundlessly inquisitive nature some of us possess may prove to be our collective downfall, he is impressed that we continue to inquire anyway. "To be able to envisage possibilities of self-destruction, yet press home the debate with the unknown, is no mean thing."

Steiner believes some forms of inquiry (though he doesn't say which) are in many respects a boon, because they enable us to "get certain perplexities into focus." And he says that "hope may lie in that small exercise." Though I agree it's necessary to get perplexities into focus, I don't think it's sufficient. Once they're in focus, the great exercise is to decide what course we should take next.

As in Athens during the days of Socrates, today we find ourselves in what the classical Greek scholar E. R. Dodds describes as a "great age of rationalism, marked by scientific advances beyond anything that earlier times had thought possible, and confronting mankind with the prospect of a society more open than any it has ever known." But, just as in ancient Greece, today we are experiencing "the unmistakable symptoms of a recoil from that prospect." Perhaps, as Dodds believes, the best an examiner of human nature can do is "remind his readers that once before a civilized people rode to this jump—rode to it and refused it." To Dodds, if we are going to stand a chance of making the jump this time around, we must first examine the demise of ancient Athens and discover an answer to this question: "Was it the horse that refused, or the rider?" His hunch is that "it was the horse—in other words, those irrational elements in human nature which govern without our knowledge so much of our behavior and so much of what we think is our thinking."

As society today makes its way along a path strikingly similar to that of ancient Athens, we seem to be approaching that same precipice, where we must either jump or recoil. Like Steiner, Dodds seems to think there is reason to hope we'll fare better this time around. We seem, on the whole, to have more tools at our disposal that better enable us to fathom our nature and come to grips with, and overcome, its irrational side. Our heightened capacity in this regard, asserts Dodds, "seems to offer the hope that if we use it wisely we shall eventually understand our horse better; that, understanding him better, we shall be able by better training to overcome his fears; and that through the overcoming of fear horse and rider will one day take that decisive jump, and take it successfully."

It'll come as no surprise that I think one of the most fruitful ways for steeling us to take the jump is the Socratic method. It enables us to bring into better focus, and then to resolve, our perplexities. Not once and for all, to be sure, because new perplexities always present themselves. But in a way that can make us more knowledgeable and at the same time more empathetic and insightful—more virtuous, Socrates might say.

I have not come across any contemporary philosopher who has formulated our predicament, and our challenge in dealing with it, with more insight and eloquence than Suzanne Langer, a longtime professor of philosophy at Connecticut College who developed a fundamental theory of symbolism that attempted to explain the meaning and cognitive import of art. In *Philosophical Sketches*, she presents it this way:

The problem of restoring the mental balance which humanity has obviously lost in this age is not psychiatric, or religious, or pedagogical, but philosophical. . . . What we need today is . . . a generation of vigorous thinkers, fiercely devoted to philosophy . . . prepared to learn whatever special skill or knowledge they may find needful—trained as fully as any scientists, without evasion of dry subjects or stepwise procedures—people who can tackle terrible questions and fight through all the misconceptions and confusing traditions that mix up our thoughts and our lives.

**Christopher
Phillips**

In short, we need a new generation of philosophers steeped in the Socratic method and ethos. But I don't understand why Langer labels as "terrible" those questions these philosophers will be charged to address. I don't think any question ipso facto has to be terrible. I read once in a daily newspaper a story about a devoted husband and father of five children who was killed by an initiate in a gang while he was washing his car. The reporter wrote that his children now were "asking such terrible questions as, 'My daddy is a good person, so why did they kill him?' and 'Where is my daddy now?'"

The tragedy itself was terrible, but the questions were not. So what we need, I think, are philosophers who will also "fight through the misconceptions" that lead us to mistake as "terrible" those vital questions that cry out to be addressed in a meaningful way.

"Is it possible to be too curious?" I again ask the Philosophers Club members. As I look at their wise, inquisitive young faces, I think to myself that I am conversing with the new generation of philosophical inquirers of whom historians will one day write glorious things. The time is ripe for such a development. As Suzanne Langer notes, "great periods of philosophy" have always come on the heels of "periods of fast cultural growth or novel experience," and we are experiencing both in great measure. In spite of considerable evidence to the contrary, I believe with Langer that somehow good just might prevail, that a new generation of philosophers will "stretch" the human mind and provide us with a "more or less general reorientation in the world," a "new development" in our "feeling for nature and each other."

Is it possible to be too curious?

"Maybe it's a question we shouldn't try to answer," Carmen of the Philosophers Club said finally in response to my query after giving the matter a great deal of thought. But then she quickly added, "But I can't *help* it. If someone asks me a question, or if I think up a question, I feel like I *have* to try to answer it. I'm *too* curious!"

Too curious.

I think of Socrates. In Plato's *Apology*, Socrates had this to say to his persecutors: "All I do as I go about is try to persuade you, both young and old, to make your first and chief concern the improvement of your soul. . . ."

Socrates so loved the question that he preferred to die than live without it. He knew the question's potential. And he knew it possessed just as much danger as it did promise. In the wrong hands, he knew it could lead to doom, and in the right hands, to salvation of a sort. But he knew that there were no guarantees, and that even the most well-intentioned questioning can have unforeseen consequences—perhaps wonderful, perhaps tragic, possibly both.

Still, the greatest danger of all, Socrates knew, was to try to dispense with the question altogether. His persecutors felt his type of questioning was subversive. They were right. If they had allowed themselves to become smitten with it, their lives would have been thrown into glorious upheaval. Their civilization might have taken a much more redemptive and fruitful turn than the freefall it took.

His persecutors' preferred brand of questioning was one in which they already had the authoritative answers to the questions posed. They duped themselves into thinking they knew the truth, and they weren't about to let anyone make them appear to be less than all-knowing sages. Socrates made it all too clear that their "Emperor's New Clothes" brand of wisdom was wearing thin. Unlike these false prophets, he could not cry "Peace! Peace!" when there was no peace.

Too curious?

Socrates didn't just question for the sake of questioning. He questioned out of conviction. He questioned in order to become the best human being possible. He was considered heretical, iconoclastic, subversive. And he was all of these things. Guilty as charged. If only all of us shared and shouldered his guilt.

Laszlo Versenyi says it is precisely because of Socrates' striving for excellence—his "superior character and insight"—that he was "powerless against the ignorance and wrongdoing of others and [had] to fall."

"If this is true," he writes, "wisdom and virtue acquire a tragic dimension, for Socrates' fate would indicate that our world is so constructed that a man of excellence is necessarily homeless in it and has to perish at the hands of those who, though inferior, dominate it to the detriment of us all."

SEEKING IGNORANCE

"Does anyone have the right to be ignorant?"

The query comes from a student sprawled on a sofa that has seen better days. The question wafts my way as I try to find my center of gravity on an off-balance chair. John, the inquisitor, has long curly red hair which seems to be off limits to a comb. His pale oval face features a universe of freckles. His jet black eyes stand out in stark relief. He has a thick leather studded collar around his neck; the kind I've seen on many a bulldog over the years.

I am facilitating my first Socrates Café in a small semi-enclosed room at the far end of a spacious café situated in a community college in Northern California. I have arrived early, as I typically do when I facilitate at a new venue; I'm always a bit worried that I'll get lost and will be late. When I arrive, I see that several others are already on hand. Instead of a stool, I have been provided with a slightly off-balance director's chair. I smile gamely at my fellow strangers as I try my best to perch myself comfortably on the chair, which tilts precariously to the right.

It's not time for the discussion to get under way, but for some reason I'd feel silly saying to him, "Let's wait to discuss your question when Socrates Café officially gets under way in ten minutes." Besides, by this time, twelve others have already shown up. They all seem intrigued by John's question.

In fact, before I even have a chance to respond, a woman whose booming voice belies her diminutive stature, says, "I don't think we have a right to be ignorant. I think we have a responsibility to constantly educate ourselves, to make ourselves less ignorant."

Then another woman, who is an elementary school student-teacher, says, "Well, as much as I might wish we don't have the right to be ignorant, I think we do. I don't see anything in the Declaration of Independence, the Constitution, or the Bill of Rights with the injunction 'Thou shall not be ignorant.' But having said that, I think in a democratic society like ours, in order to be fully involved in it, we should feel an *obligation* to become less and less ignorant. Which means, at least to me, like she said, that we must continually educate ourselves."

"I love the wide-eyed look of exuberance of children who discover the joys of learning, and as a consequence become less ignorant," says a woman who is a part-time student and works part-time at the college's day care center for employees and students. "And yet they retain such an innocence. Education is a process of making us less ignorant without necessarily making us jaded. In fact it can endow us with an even greater sense of wonder. And wonder, I think, is a form of innocence."

"Is all education a process of making someone less ignorant?" I ask her. "It seems that you can be 'educated' to believe that white people are superior, for instance, or you can be 'educated' to think that only people who subscribe to certain beliefs are going to heaven—and such 'education' only feeds and foments ignorance."

The teacher mulls this over for a moment before replying, "That's true. So I think I need to amend what I said earlier and say that education at its best is a process of making us less ignorant. And at its worst, education is a mockery of what education is supposed to be all about, and can actually make you 'less educated,' which is the same thing as being 'more ignorant.' I think this latter type of education isn't really education at all, but is 'indoctrination' or 'brainwashing.'"

"So educating people to be more open-minded, to be lifelong critical thinkers, is not a form of indoctrination?" I ask.

"It is," says a middle-aged man. Before he explains himself further, he tells us that this is his first time on campus today, that he was looking into pursuing studies in sociology after taking a thirty-year hiatus from school, and that it was just by happenstance that he passed by the café, where our discussion was set to begin, as he was making his way back to his car in the parking lot. "It's a good type of indoctrination, because it leads you to realize that there's no such thing as the answer in any area of knowledge.

It leads you to realize that you'll always be ignorant of so much more than you'll know. And by robbing you of your innocence of this fact, it inspires you to keep learning all your life."

"What's the difference between ignorance and innocence?" I ask the group.

"You can be both ignorant and innocent. In fact, more often than not I think they go hand in glove—but they're not the same thing," says a frail man with tiny blue eyes and a bushy mustache that threatens to envelop the entire lower region of his face. He has just enrolled in college this semester after a lifetime of auto-didactic learning. "I think it's good to be ignorant of some things," he says. "I've taken a lot of risks with my life. And when I look back on the decisions I've made, I realize that if I knew then what I know now, I'd probably never have had the courage to take these risks, though they enabled me to live a thrilling life in which I traveled all over the world. So it was good to be ignorant and innocent."

"I think you're confusing the concepts ignorance and innocence," another participant says to him. "You weren't ignorant when you took these risks, because you didn't intentionally put on blinders to prevent yourself from knowing certain things that might have made you think twice about doing the things you did. But you *were* innocent of the potential pitfalls. So, you can choose to be ignorant, but you're *naturally* innocent. There's no choice to innocence. For instance, until you experience the grief over the loss of a loved one, you're innocent about what such an experience would be like. But if someone ever tried to explain to you what such grief is like and you closed yourself off to this person, then you'd have purposely chosen to be ignorant."

"I think that no one would choose to be ignorant," says an elderly woman sitting next to the young schoolteacher. "I think that it is our nature to desire to know everything we can, because knowledge is good."

"I disagree," says a man who identifies himself as a history professor. "I don't think we all have a desire to know. Some cultures seem to bask in their innocence. And many Western intellectuals think such innocence is a great thing. For instance, Rousseau glorified and romanticized the innocence of primitive cultures. But if these cultures had been less innocent of the ways of conquering nations, they probably wouldn't be living in the wretched conditions of exploitation so many of them live in today. Many of these cultures seemed to want to be 'kept in the dark' about such things.

"However, having said that," he goes on to say, "I do not think that all knowledge is good. Sometimes ignorance is a very good thing." He pauses, as if deciding whether he should explain himself. Then, his brow furrowing, he says, " I never told my mother that my dad, her husband, died. Because I felt it would be too devastating for her. Dad has been dead several months now, and Mom is on the edge of senility. She still doesn't know. I think it's best if she remains ignorant of this."

There is a long lull. No one seems quite to know what, if anything, to say next.

"I think it's even worse when people aren't ignorant of certain things and yet still act with ignorance," John finally offers. "For instance, when a racist continues to be a racist, yet is aware of the reasons why he's a racist—perhaps he's even aware that his racism is illogical because he knows damn well that all of us are 99.9 percent genetically identical—then that's even more scary than when people are racist out of sheer ignorance."

"It seems like we're distinguishing between willful and unwillful ignorance, what someone earlier referred to as 'intentionality,'" says a student who is scrunched into a small space on the same sofa on which John is sprawled. "It seems that at any given point in our lives, we're ignorant of tons of things. In order to do A, we have to turn a blind eye to B, C, D . . ."

"You're so right," says a man who is leaning against a wall in a far-off corner and now approaches the group. He identifies himself as the dean of student affairs. "In fact," he then says, "if I tried to do everything I'd like to do, I'd probably never accomplish much of anything because I'd be stretching myself so thin. So maybe the best we can do is to be aware of our ignorance, but not to accept that we always have to be as ignorant as we are now."

"I think that was Socrates' philosophy," the history professor then says. "And the reason I think he was the wisest man who ever lived is because he recognized just how ignorant he was. Every time he interrogated a Sophist, even though he said he was seeking knowledge from them, he really was seeking out their ignorance—because in every instance, the Sophists clearly didn't know what they claimed to know. So Socrates concluded that there's hardly any knowledge at all, but a whole lot of ignorance."

Then he looks at me for an uncomfortably long time. Finally he says with a wry smile, "I think you're seeking ignorance, just like Socrates did."

THE SOCRATIC SENSIBILITY

It was time to wrap up our dialogue, so this last comment was left unchallenged. But it stayed with me long after the dialogue ended. Over the years I've heard many others say variations of the same thing as this history professor—namely, that Socrates was seeking ignorance because he claimed he didn't know anything authoritatively. But I don't think this is so. There's a big difference between claiming to know something and claiming to know something authoritatively. Socrates falls in the first camp. He'd never make a claim like "I know because I don't know." I think he'd have considered such a statement disingenuous at best. Socrates was intensely committed to the task of discovering what it was to be an excellent human being, and he did teach people a specific way, or method, of becoming more and more enlightened about how to become more virtuous. Many philosophers ever since, from Hume to Descartes to Wittgenstein to Russell, have taken this "skeptical attitude"—what I call this Socratic sensibility—as their own launching pad for gaining insight into many of life's most vexing conundrums. And this sensibility has always been associated with the most searching and penetrating analyses of the great philosophers.

All who adopt this sensibility are unwilling to accept conclusions unless there are very convincing grounds for them. A Zen master might exhort you, 'Don't think: Look!" because when you're thinking, you're trying to understand instead of bathing yourself in direct experience. But Socrates would exhort you: "Look. And think. Then look some more. And think some more. Don't ever stop looking, or thinking." He would maintain that thinking is a form of looking, a form of direct experience. If you look without thinking, then that would be intentional ignorance, a kind of blindness. But if you look and think, if you observe and think, and also listen to others' perspectives on what they observe and think, then you'll still be ignorant, but not quite as ignorant. You'll have inched a little further along the Socratic version of the path of enlightenment.

And by inching along in this fashion, by seeking the truth gropingly, you become less and less ignorant. You gain what might be called wisdom of a certain sort, "Socratic wisdom," which amounts to this: You are better able to determine what you do know—what stands up to rigorous scrutiny—and what you do not know. You become aware of the existing limits of your knowledge, but in a way that inspires you to push those limits further and further outward. As Richard Tarnas puts it, for Socrates "the discovery of ignorance was just the beginning of the philosophical task," not the end. After discovering one's ignorance, one can then "begin to overcome one's received assumptions that obscured the true nature of what it was to be a human being." Socrates was reviled by many Athenians for showing them how murky and confused was their use of such concepts as courage, justice, the good, and virtue. They resented his insistence on critically analyzing the exact meaning of propositions and determining the precise extent to which they were true. Yet reflective examination, among other things, can show us that some errors stem from inaccurate knowledge, others from faulty reasoning, and still others from careless use of language.

To this day, Socrates' example continues to teach us how to expand our own intellectual and imaginative horizons. He was extremely critical of those who let other people do their thinking for them. He saw his role as akin to that of a midwife; he helped people give birth to their own ideas, and to work through the particular beliefs by which they could choose to live.

TRUE TEACHING

Above all, Socrates has passed on to us the conviction that we must be willing to subject our beliefs radically and continually to encounter upon encounter, from without and from within. Socrates engaged in what Laszlo Versenyi describes as "true teaching," the centerpiece of which is "a questioning of accepted opinions, an examination of beliefs, a refutation of dogmas, a testing of knowledge and an indictment of ignorance."

Christopher Phillips

It is humbling, to be sure, for a person to discover that much of what he thought he knew was based on a foundation of quicksand. But as Socrates says in Plato's *Theaetetus*, "If you should ever conceive again . . . your budding thoughts should be better as a result of this scrutiny. . . ." In Plato's *Meno*, Socrates first catechized the young slave in such a way that he came to realize he didn't know what he thought he knew. Socrates didn't do this to make the boy look silly, much less to discourage him from learning. To the contrary, as Socrates himself explains in *Meno*, "By making him perplexed and giving him a shock we haven't done him any harm . . . rather, we've helped him toward finding the truth, for now he'll search gladly, seeing. . . . But do you think he would have tried to search and to acquire knowledge while he thought he knew what he did not know, before he was reduced to the perplexity of being aware that he did not know and this yearning for knowledge? . . . Now, because of his loss, he will find out something, searching with me. . . ."

"*Sed omnia praeclara tam difficilia quam rara sunt*," Spinoza writes at the end of his *Ethics:* "Everything excellent is as difficult as it is rare." Yet our ideas of "excellence" today seem all too often tied to the acquisition of material wealth. But it is neither exceedingly difficult nor rare for shrewd investors with considerable money to begin with to rake in gobs more money in a bullish economy. Nor is it difficult, or rare, for today's philosopher-sophists, just as in the days of Socrates, to "counsel" the wealthy that virtually *any* goal they set for themselves and then go on to accomplish is "excellent." They steer clear at all costs from Socrates' view that "virtue does not come from wealth, but . . . wealth and every good thing that men have . . . comes from virtue."

In my travels, I've even encountered a few academic philosophers who philosophize with private "clients" at hefty hourly rates. Some seem threatened that I don't aim to profit from philosophizing with the public; and they resent that I show people, many of whom never have and never will take a university course in philosophy, how to facilitate discussions themselves using the Socratic method. They want all "public philosophers" to have graduate degrees in philosophy, and to be "certified"; and they want to charge tidy sums for such certification. To them, it's vital that the general public philosophize only with a specialist, and at a cost.

I've encountered some today who, like the fee-charging Sophists of old, take pains to disparage Socrates himself. They maintain that if Socrates earned no wages from his philosophizing, then he already had money or was propped up by wealthy friends, a classic sophism. It's easy to say that only the rich or their coterie can afford to give short shrift to purely moneymaking endeavors; but it is a great insult to the countless people who disavow material gain in order to devote their lives to higher causes. And Plato's *Apology* makes crystal clear that Socrates willingly lived in extreme poverty in order to stay true to his ideals.

Socrates engaged in a lifelong pursuit of a type of excellence that no amount of money could buy. Of the wealthy who might inspire to be his patrons today, I'd like to think he might ask: Is it possible to envision a society in which the gap between rich and poor is much less dramatic than it is now? Are you responsible for the well-being of your fellow humans? What is more important, the way you earn your money or the fact that you are successful at it? What is "success"? Is it still "excellent" if the corporations responsible for your windfall are responsible for environmental degradation and labor exploitation?

HUMAN EXCELLENCE

Christopher Phillips

To Socrates, an excellent human being is one who strives to acquire certain virtues, such as temperance, courage, and wisdom. Why? Because the acquisition of such virtues creates a different kind of wealth—a wealth of empathy, of imaginative vision, of self-discovery.

Implicit within the "Socratic virtues" is this injunction: You can only attain human excellence if you also strive to make it possible for your fellow humans to do so too. To embrace this injunction requires both a social conscience and an imaginative vision that has always been difficult and rare.

In the *Apology*, his fate in the balance, Socrates has this to say to his fellow Athenians:

> As long as I breathe and have the strength to go on, I won't quit philosophizing, I won't quit exhorting you and whomever I happen to meet, in my customary way: Esteemed friend, citizen of Athens, the greatest city in the world, so outstanding in both intelligence and power, aren't you ashamed to care so much to make all the money you can, and to advance your reputation and prestige—while for truth and wisdom and the improvement of your soul you have no care or worry?

To Socrates, a person "should only consider whether, in doing anything, he is doing right or wrong—acting the part of a good man or bad."

At the end of Plato's *Phaedo*, the moving dialogue that describes the final moments of Socrates' life, his closest friends visit him in his prison cell. Just before he drinks the hemlock, they ask him what they can do to "be of most service" to him. Socrates has just one request: he bids them to continue to "follow that path of life" which they have discovered, over the course of many rich dialogues together, makes life worth living.

**SOCRATES
CAFÉ**

GLOSSARY OF
PHILOSOPHERS

ANAXAGORAS (c. 500–428 B.C.). The first of the Greek philosophers to move to Athens, and the first to be tried formally on a charge of heresy or impiety. Anaxagoras held that everything consists of an infinite number of particles or seeds or elemental "stuffs," and that in all things there is a portion of everything.

ARENDT, HANNAH (1906–1975). German-born philosopher and one of the century's leading political theorists who, fleeing Nazi persecution, went to France in 1933 and then came to America in 1940. Arendt believed that meaningful action hinges on careful and deliberative thought. She served on the faculty of the University of Chicago from 1963 to 1967 and then at the New School for Social Research in New York. One of her most well-known works, *The Origins of Totalitarianism*, linked the rise of totalitarianism to nineteenth-century anti-Semitism and imperialism.

ARISTOTLE (384–322 B.C.). Pupil of Plato, tutor to Alexander the Great, and founder of the Lyceum in Athens. A philosopher of wide-ranging interests, Aristotle is widely considered to be the first to glean the many implicit aspects of knowledge. He recognized the critical function of definition, induction, and deduction in the development of science, and he marked off the sciences into three areas: the theoretical, which strived for truth; the practical, which was action-oriented; and the productive, which aimed at creating.

Christopher
Phillips

BRADLEY, FRANCIS HERBERT (1846–1924). British idealist philosopher who held that Truth, as set forth in language, could never wholly capture "the whole" or "Absolute" totality of things. As with all absolute idealists, Bradley held that the difference between subject and object is only a formal one, and is simply the work of thought.

BUCHLER, JUSTUS (1915–1991). Naturalist philosopher who developed a groundbreaking metaphysics of natural complexes. Buchler, who joined the Columbia University faculty in 1937 and was its chairman from 1964 to 1967, was considered the moral and intellectual leader of Columbia's acclaimed contemporary civilization program. He later founded a graduate program in philosophical perspectives at the State University of New York at Stony Brook.

CLIFFORD, WILLIAM KINGDON (1845–1879). British mathematician and scientific philosopher. Clifford wrote acclaimed essays on the theory of knowledge, ethics, and religion, and strove to provide an interpretation of life in the light of the latest scientific findings.

DEMOCRITUS OF ABDERA (460–370 B.C.). Along with Leucippus, his teacher, the prime exponent of the philosophy known as atomism. Democritus was a younger contemporary of Socrates and an older contemporary of Plato. He believed in a mechanistic universe devoid of any design or purpose and, like Leucippus, postulated that everything is a plurality of particles or corpuscles that have varying sizes and shapes as they clump together but that do not differ in qualitative makeup.

DESCARTES, RENÉ (1596–1650). French mathematician considered the father of modern philosophy. Descartes attempted to extend the mathematical method, with its certain and self-evident proofs, in order to acquire irrefutable knowledge about the world. Launching his investigation from a standpoint of universal skepticism, he concluded that the only thing that was true beyond a shadow of a doubt was his own thinking; hence his maxim "I think, therefore I am." This first-person foundation to his theory of knowledge led his acolytes to institutionalize the famous Cartesian dualism in which mind and matter were separated into two wholly different yet interacting substances.

DEWEY, JOHN (1859–1952). A leading American philosopher, political theorist, educator, and social reformer. Throughout his career, Dewey emphasized the paramount importance of inquiry in gaining knowledge. At the same time, though, he asserted that his Western philosophical forebears had erred in focusing primarily on abstract, transcendent, and a priori systems of knowledge, metaphysics, and methods of inquiry. To Dewey, inquiry was a self-corrective process, conducted in specific historical and cultural or "practical" circumstances and contexts, that led to a type of knowledge that could always be further amended and refined and evolved.

EPICTETUS (c. 50–c. 138). Stoic moral philosopher who established a school of philosophy after being freed as a slave. Epictetus believed that the purpose of philosophy was not to gain public accolades but rather to become a better citizen of the world.

FOUCAULT, MICHEL (1926–1984). French philosopher and social critic who developed an approach to intellectual history that he coined the "archaeology of knowledge." Foucault sought to investigate and root out the implicit knowledge and systems of thought that underpinned specific practices, institutions, and theories.

GILSON, ETIENNE (1884–1978). French Catholic philosopher, historian of medieval philosophy, and radical theologian. Gilson attempted to resuscitate Thomas Aquinas' distinction between essence and existence in created being, and to assert the primacy of existence in any account of being.

HEGEL, GEORG WILHELM FRIEDRICH (1770–1831). German philosopher whose great philosophical system of metaphysics continues to wield a great influence on philosophy. To Hegel, the subject matter of philosophy is reality as a whole, which he referred to as the Absolute. Most Hegel scholars describe his metaphysical system as a dialectical scheme of thesis, antithesis, and synthesis. His system charts the development or progress of world history and of ideas towards an ever-higher synthesis that leads toward knowledge of the Absolute *Geist*, which is translated as both "mind" and "spirit."

Christopher Phillips

HEIDEGGER, MARTIN (1889–1976). German philosopher and critic of modernity and democracy. Heidegger strove to understand the nature of "being," particularly as it relates to how humans act in and relate to the world.

HERACLITUS (c. 500 B.C.). Pre-Socratic Greek philosopher whose philosophical perspectives survived only in fragmented text, which later authors quoted and attributed to him in memorable aphorisms. These aphorisms emphasized unity in the world of change. Heraclitus apparently believed that fire was the source of natural substances and that the world is governed by *logos*, which is loosely translated as "the word or thing said."

HOBBES, THOMAS (1588–1679). One of the founders of modern political philosophy. Hobbes attempted to make a science of politics with the aim of putting an end to political turmoil. In his landmark work *Leviathan*, Hobbes attacked the Church of England, endorsing the practice of religion free of state and ecclesiastical authority, and he developed a "philosophy of natural equality" in which he held that all men by nature are equal in physical and mental capabilities.

HUME, DAVID (1711–1776). Scottish historian, essayist, and leading empiricist philosopher. Hume was a central figure in the Enlightenment, famous for his arguments against the proofs for God's existence. In his *Treatise of Human Nature*, Hume attempted to use introspective and observational investigations to study the human mind and give an account of knowledge and belief, morality, and such "passions" as love and hate and humility and vice. He argued that there was no such thing as a priori principles that are presupposed or innately known rather than derived from experience of actual events.

JAMES, WILLIAM (1842–1910). American philosopher, psychologist, Harvard professor, and popularizer of pragmatism. James expanded the application of pragmatism beyond the original areas given to it by its founder, Charles Sanders Peirce, to develop an account or theory of truth and to try to reconcile seeming conflicts between science and values. For James, the truth of an idea is determined by its social or ethical utility and import or its ethical consequences.

KANT, IMMANUEL (1724–1804). German philosopher whose influential "critical philosophy" asserted that ideas do not necessarily conform to the external world, but rather the world is known only to the extent to which it conforms with the human mind's structure. In his famous categorical imperative, Kant exhorted people, as moral agents, to act in such a way that their action is commanded for its own sake—as if it were a universal law of nature—with no view to some end it is supposed to bring about. Kant held that a moral person had to believe in God, freedom, and morality, even though there was no provable scientific or metaphysical foundation on which to base this belief. Kant built a comprehensive theory of knowledge, aesthetics, and ethics that influenced almost all subsequent philosophy.

KAUFMANN, WALTER (1921–1980). German-born professor of philosophy at Princeton University from 1947 until his death. Kaufmann is primarily known for his translations of many of the works of Friedrich

Nietzsche, and of Goethe's *Faust*, but he also produced a great many original works, including books on existentialism and religion. Kaufmann outspokenly lamented the dearth of the Socratic ethos and the pervasive "microscopism" in academic philosophy.

Christopher
Phillips

KIERKEGAARD, SØREN (1813–1855). Danish philosopher, theologian, and social critic. Kierkegaard was the first philosopher to be labeled an existentialist. His philosophical stance/attitude was exemplified by his dissatisfaction with traditional philosophy as superficial, overly pedantic, and far removed from pressing life concerns, his refusal to be labeled, and his rejection of any set of beliefs.

LANGER, SUZANNE (1895–1985). American philosopher who characterizes humans as "symbolic" beings and finds in symbolism a "new key" in philosophy. Langer studied the "transformative" role of symbols in the structuring of works of art, as well as in symbolic logic, the natural sciences, and psychoanalysis. Langer also made significant contributions in philosophy of language and philosophy of mind.

LEIBNIZ, GOTTFRIED WILHELM (1646–1716). Eminent German rationalist philosopher who, along with Sir Isaac Newton, was an inventor of calculus and a forefather of modern mathematical logic. Advocating the principle that reason is primary in any explanation, Leibniz held that there are an infinite number of possible worlds, all of which God considered before creating the actual world, which is one large system revealing God's plan and is "the best of the possible worlds." Leibniz believed that there is a sufficient reason why everything that is in the world *is* in the world and why it is just the way it is.

LEUCIPPUS (fifth century B.C.). Early Greek philosopher, teacher of Democritus, and founder of atomism, a theory in which the physical world is composed of an infinite number of indivisible particles or corpuscles moving randomly in an infinite void and differing in size and shape but in no qualitative way.

LOCKE, JOHN (1632–1704). Influential founder of British empiricism. Locke held that there is no such thing as innate ideas, but rather that experience is the foundation for all human understanding. He set forth his political theory in *Two Treatises of Government,* asserting that men are, "by nature, all free, equal and independent." Believing that philosophy was virtually inseparable from the sciences, in his *Essay Concerning Human Understanding* Locke attempted to reconcile knowledge with the latest findings of seventeenth-century science.

MARCUS AURELIUS (121–180). Roman emperor and philosopher, and a proponent of Stoicism, a system of ethics essentially guided by the notion that a moral life is one that is led in accordance with nature and is controlled by virtue. His *Meditations* reflect on life, death, conduct, and the cosmos, and often emphasize the insignificance of human life.

MERLEAU-PONTY, MAURICE (1908–1961). French philosopher concerned primarily with the "phenomenology of perception" (also the title of his major work). Drawing on empirical psychology and physiology as well as the work of such German philosophers as Heidegger, Merleau-Ponty emphasized the way in which human experience is necessarily a way of being in the world rather than of shutting oneself off from the world.

MONTAIGNE, MICHEL EYQUEM DE (1533–1592). French philosopher and essayist known as the French Socrates. In his *Apology for Raymond Sebond* (1580), Montaigne defended the Spanish monk's attempt to demonstrate that Catholic beliefs could be firmly established by reason, using Sebond's views as a springboard for his skeptical argument. This essay made Montaigne the guiding force of skepticism and cultural relativism in modern Europe. Montaigne gained particular renown for his witty and humane yet mordantly incisive literary work *Essais.*

NAGEL, ERNEST (1901–1985). An American philosopher born in

Austria-Hungry, known for his work on the implications of science. Nagel was a member of Columbia University's department of philosophy for over forty years and was eventually designated University Professor, the school's most distinguished rank. He is best known for his *Structure of Science*, which demonstrated the logic of scientific explanation as it developed in all the sciences.

Christopher
Phillips

NIETZSCHE, FRIEDRICH WILHELM (1844–1900). German classical philologist, poet, social critic, and philosopher. Nietzsche attacked traditional metaphysics and morality and heralded the "Superman" or "overman," a "deep-souled" type who, he claimed, embodied a life-affirming "will to power." Nietzsche rejected the notion of absolute knowledge. He believed that all thinking is limited by one's perspectives, and maintained that everything is an interpretation and that all knowledge is provisional in character.

PEIRCE, CHARLES SANDERS (1839–1914). American philosopher and scientist who described himself as a "laboratory philosopher." Peirce was known as the originator of pragmatism. He held that beliefs are "rules for action" and that ideas should be evaluated pragmatically, or in terms of their consequences, and that these consequences alone constitute their meaning. He also made pioneering philosophical investigations into the logic of relations and of truth functions.

PLATO (c. 428–c. 348 B.C.) Athenian philosopher and pupil of Socrates. Many of his dialogues feature Socrates as an indefatigable questioner whose "elenctic" method of interrogation or cross-examination often reveals the false claims to knowledge made by many of the most revered Sophists of ancient Greece. Plato is widely considered the originator, and unsurpassed practitioner, of philosophical discourse as we know it today.

PYTHAGORAS (c. 582–507 B.C.). Philosopher, mathematician, and sage. Pythagoras was founder of a quasi-religious brotherhood—which still existed 150 years later in Plato's time—that believed in the immortality and transmigration of the soul and the kinship of all life.

RANDALL, JOHN HERMAN, JR. (1899–1980). American naturalist philosopher, historian of philosophy and the intellectual tradition. Randall was acclaimed as an interpreter of Greek humanism and Christian ethics. The son of a Baptist minister, he taught for more than half a century at Columbia University. Randall, an outspoken scholar-activist who often engaged in philosophical inquiry with the general public, was an influential proponent of naturalism, a philosophical school that relates the scientific method to philosophy and holds that all beings and events in the universe are natural.

ROUSSEAU, JEAN-JACQUES (1712–1778). Swiss-born French thinker influential in political philosophy, educational theory, and the Romantic movement. Rousseau argued in one of his earlier works that society is the culprit for all of humankind's ills. But in his landmark work *The Social Contract*, Rousseau—captivated by the civic ideal of the ancient Roman republic—maintained that governments, at their best, were manifestations of their citizens' rational choices for the common good (what he called "general will").

RUSSELL, BERTRAND (1872–1970). English radical political advocate and pacifist essayist and philosopher best known for his work in logic and the philosophy of mathematics (he held that all mathematics could be derived from logical premises). Russell influenced generations of general readers by writing on a variety of topics—including education, religion, science, and history—and he was awarded the Nobel Prize for Literature in 1950. His collaboration with Alfred North Whitehead on *Principia Mathematica* precipitated the development of modern logic.

RYLE, GILBERT (1900–1976). English philosopher and classicist whose landmark *Concept of Mind* critiques and debunks Descartes' mind-body duality. Along with Wittgenstein, Ryle was one of the leading philosophers of the middle period of twentieth-century language philosophy.

SANTAYANA, GEORGE (1863–1952). Spanish-born American philosopher, poet, essayist, and novelist who joined the faculty at Harvard University in 1889. A student of William James and Josiah Royce, Santayana held that all reality is external to consciousness and that all beliefs about the external world are ultimately based on "animal faith." In his five-volume *Life of Reason,* Santayana unified science, religion, and art by characterizing each as a singular but equally valid form of symbolism.

SARTRE, JEAN-PAUL (1905–1980). Renowned existentialist philosopher, novelist, playwright, and social critic. His philosophical investigations focused on the nature of human life and the structure of consciousness. Sartre maintained that the essence of human existence is the capacity for choice. He consequently concluded that humans are "condemned to be free," and that those who do not accept responsibility for their actions are acting in "bad faith."

SCHOPENHAUER, ARTHUR (1788–1860). German philosopher and prose writer who held that all reality essentially is will—a ceaseless, largely unconscious striving that reveals itself in sundry ways and that invariably leads to suffering. He believed it would be better never to have existed at all than to suffer, and was labeled a pessimist for his views on suffering. Schopenhauer, who worked outside the academic mainstream, systematically sets forth his metaphysical system in his *The World as Will and Representation.*

SOCRATES (c. 469–399 B.C.). Son of a stonemason and a midwife, mentor of Plato. Socrates was tried and executed at age seventy on charges of impiety and corrupting Athens' youth. He apparently did not write anything, and yet he is considered the most memorable and influential of philosophers. His paradigmatic quest for human excellence and his

Christopher
Phillips

belief that "the unexamined life is not worth living" continue to serve as beacons for many.

SPINOZA, BARUCH (OR BENEDICT) DE (1632–1677). Dutch-born philosopher renowned for his frugality and courageous stances. In 1656 Spinoza was briefly expelled from the Jewish community in Amsterdam as a heretic. In 1673 the Reformed Church condemned, and subsequently banned, Spinoza for espousing tolerance and peace in his *Tractatus Theologico-Politicus.* Countering Descartes, Spinoza developed in his *Ethics* a philosophy of monism in which he asserted that mind and body are facets of a single substance called God or nature. He used a mathematical system of deductive reasoning to present his views.

THALES (c. 585 B.C.). Greek statesman, geometer, astonomer, and sage. Thales is generally deemed the first Western philosopher. He lived in Miletus in Asia Minor, and apparently believed that water is the fundamental element of the world.

THOMAS AQUINAS (1225–1274), Italian philosopher and theologian considered the greatest of the Scholastics. Aquinas is thought by many to be the most influential philosopher of the medieval era. He gained renown for reconciling Aristotle's philosophy with Christian doctrine to create the orthodox Catholic philosophy.

UNAMUNO, MIGUEL DE (1864–1936). Spanish writer, philologist, and philosopher. Virtually all his writings dealt with the meaning of life and death. Unamuno developed a "tragic sense of life" that maintained that even if we cannot be sure our life has any sort of transcendent or otherworldly significance, we should act as if it does.

VLASTOS, GREGORY (1907–1991). Professor of philosophy at Berkeley and at Princeton, and noted scholar of Socrates and Plato. Vlastos espoused a doctrine of egalitarianism, holding that each person has the same "individual human worth."

VOLTAIRE (FRANÇOIS MARIE AROUET) (1694–1778). French philosopher, essayist, novelist, and social critic. This politically engaged liberal humanist was one of the most prominent thinkers of the Enlightenment. His classic satire *Candide* derides the view of Leibniz that no matter how evil an action or occurrence, "all is for the best in the best of all possible worlds." Voltaire believed that we must take concrete action to combat and thwart the evil in this world. "We must cultivate our garden," he wrote.

WHITEHEAD, ALFRED NORTH (1861–1947). British mathematician and philosopher. Whitehead sought to develop a systematic metaphysics of nature based on modern physics and logic. Whitehead was the tutor of Bertrand Russell in Cambridge, where he was a fellow of Trinity from 1884 to 1910. He then was professor of philosophy at Harvard from 1924 to 1937.

WITTGENSTEIN, LUDWIG (1889–1951). Austrian-born philosopher who is considered one of the most influential philosophers of the century. Wittgenstein emphasized the importance of the study of language. His landmark *Tractatus Logico-Philosophicus*, the only work published in his lifetime, developed his thoughts on the foundations of logic and mathematics and led to the development of several important fields of philosophy: logical positivism, linguistic analysis, and semantics.

XENOPHON (c. 430–355 B.C.). Greek general, moralist, and historian who depicted Socrates as a teacher of virtue and practical knowledge and tried in his writings to defend Socrates from the charges that led to his execution.

ZENO OF ELEA (c. 470 B.C.). Pre-Socratic philosopher who held that motion, change, and plurality are logical absurdities and that only an immutable being is real. In his famous paradoxes, which presented four arguments against motion, he tried to use logical demonstrations to disprove common assumptions about time and motion.

FURTHER READING

I have benefited immensely from works of mostly unheralded modern philosophers who have engaged in a version of philosophical inquiry that epitomizes the Socratic tendency. *Metaphysics of Natural Complexes* (Albany: State University of New York Press, 1990), by Justus Buchler, offers a novel and compelling "categorial theory" of metaphysics rivaling that developed by Aristotle. To grasp fully the range of Buchler's philosophical thought, one should turn to his slender works: *Charles Peirce's Empiricism* (New York: Harcourt, Brace and Company, 1939), *Nature and Judgment* (New York: Grosset & Dunlap, 1955), *Toward a General Theory of Human Judgment* (New York: Dover Publications, 1951), and *The Concept of Method* (New York: Columbia University Press, 1961). His final book, *The Main of Light: On the Concept of Poetry* (New York: Oxford University Press, 1974), offers a unique and illuminating perspective on the concept of poetry, and also presents a succinct synthesis of his seminal theory of judgment. Much can also be gleaned of Buchler's philosophical thinking, and its implications in virtually every field of knowledge, by reading *Nature's Perspectives: Prospects for Ordinal Metaphysics* (Albany:

State University of New York Press, 1991), edited by Armen Marsoobian, Kathleen Wallace, and Robert S. Corrington.

Christopher
Phillips

John Herman Randall's three-volume *Career of Philosophy* (New York: Columbia University Press, 1962, 1965, 1977) is a piercing analysis and exploration of philosophical thinking throughout the ages. His *Nature and Historical Experience: Essays in Naturalism and the Theory of History* (New York: Columbia University Press, 1958) is a philosophical tour de force. Randall's *Aristotle* (New York: Columbia University Press, 1960) and *Plato: Dramatist of the Life of Reason* (New York: Columbia University Press, 1960), offer provocative perspectives on these two philosophers, as well as Socrates, that often differ dramatically from those of most academic philosophers. In all his books, his engaging and lucid writing style is a breath of fresh air. Also well worth reading are Randall's *The Role of Knowledge in Western Religion* (Boston: Starr King Press, 1958), *How Philosophy Uses Its Past* (New York: Columbia University Press, 1963), and *The Making of the Modern Mind* (New York: Columbia University Press, 1977).

As I said near the beginning of my book, Walter Kaufmann continues to be known primarily for his translations of most of Friedrich Nietzsche's major works. Though most agree that his Nietzsche translations are uniformly excellent, I much prefer his *Nietzsche: Philosopher, Psychologist, AntiChrist* (Princeton, N.J.: Princeton University Press, 1950) to the running commentaries he included in the translated works. Most of the books Kaufmann wrote that charted new philosophical ground are out of print but well worth the effort of finding. His earliest original works, such as *The Faith of a Heretic* and *Critique of Religion and Philosophy,* are replete with memorable passages. But with the exception of his collection of essays, *From Shakespeare to Existentialism* (Princeton, N.J.: Princeton University Press, 1959), the books he wrote later in his career are of much more lasting philosophic value. His *Without*

Guilt and Justice: From Decidophobia to Autonomy (New York: Peter H. Wyden, 1973) is a thoughtful exploration of the concepts of guilt and justice. His *Man's Lot: A Trilogy* (New York: Reader's Digest Press, 1978), a combination of philosophical essays and beautiful photography (Kaufmann's own), offers a variety of perspectives on what precisely it is to be a human being throughout the history of philosophy, art, literature, and world civilization. His *Discovering the Mind* trilogy (recently reissued by Transaction Publishers, New Brunswick, N.J.)—which presents singular and even radical perspectives on such intellectual luminaries as Goethe, Kant, Hegel, Freud, Jung, and Adler—is a worthy capstone to his career.

Suzanne Langer's short *Philosophical Sketches: A Study of the Human Mind in Relation to Feeling, Explored Thought, Art, Language, and Symbol* (Baltimore: Johns Hopkins Press, 1962) is a wonderful way to segue into her philosophical work. It should also serve as a springboard to her much more involved books, including *Feeling and Form* (New York: Charles Scribner's Sons, 1953), her multivolume *Mind: An Essay on Human Feeling* (Baltimore: Johns Hopkins University Press, 1967 and 1972), and *Philosophy in a New Key* (Cambridge, Mass.: Harvard University Press, 1949).

Among other books I have particularly profited from are Ludwig Wittgenstein, *Tractatus Logico-Philosophicus* (London: Routledge and Kegan Paul, 1963); William Kingdon Clifford, *Lectures and Essays* (New York: Macmillan and Company, 1886); Morris Cohen, *Reason and Nature* (New York: Free Press, 1953) and *Reason and Law* (New York: Collier Books, 1961); Matthew Lipman, *Thinking in Education* (Cambridge, U.K., and New York: Cambridge University Press, 1991) and *What Happens in Art* (New York: Irvington Publishers, 1967); Hannah Arendt, *The Human Condition* (Chicago: University of Chicago Press, 1958), *The Life of the Mind* (New York: Harcourt Brace Jovanovich, 1978), and *Men in Dark*

Times (New York: Harcourt, Brace and World, 1958); Gilbert Ryle, *The Concept of Mind* (New York: Barnes & Noble, 1949); Ernest Nagel, *Logic Without Metaphysics and Other Studies in the Philosophy of Science* (Glencoe, Ill.: Free Press, 1956) and his magnum opus *The Structure of Science: Problems in the Logic of Scientific Explanation* (New York: Harcourt, Brace and World, 1961); E. R. Dodds, *The Ancient of Progress: and Other Essays on Greek Literature and Belief* (New York: Oxford University Press, 1973), *Pagan and Christian in an Age of Anxiety* (New York: W. W. Norton, 1970), and *The Greeks and the Irrational* (Berkeley: University of California Press, 1951); David Hume, *A Treatise of Human Nature* (Oxford: Clarendon Press, 1951); Paolo Freire, *Pedagogy of the Oppressed* (New York: Continuum Publishing Company, 1990); John Dewey, *Logic: The Theory of Inquiry* (New York: Holt, 1938); John Dewey and Arthur F. Bentley, *Knowing and the Known* (Boston: Beacon Press, 1960); Charles S. Peirce, *Philosophical Writings of Peirce* (New York: Dover Publications, 1955); and George Santayana, *Obiter Scripta* (New York: Charles Scribner's Sons, 1936) and *Selected Critical Writings of Santayana,* 2 volumes (Cambridge, U.K., and New York: Cambridge University Press, 1968); Elias Canetti, *Auto da Fé* (New York: Noonday Press, 1984); Hermann Broch, *The Guiltless* (San Francisco: North Point Press, 1987), *The Death of Virgil* (New York: Vintage Books, 1995), and *The Sleepwalkers: A Trilogy* (New York: Vintage Books, 1996); Robert Musil, *The Man Without Qualities* (New York: Knopf, 1995); Fyodor Dostoevsky, *Notes from the Underground* (New York: W. W. Norton, 1989); Ralph Ellison, *Invisible Man* (New York: Signet, 1952); Rolf Hochhuth, *The Deputy* (New York: Grove Press, 1964); Italo Calvino, *Six Memos for the Next Millennium* (Cambridge, Mass.: Harvard University Press, 1988); Robert Coles, *Children of Crisis: A Study of Courage and Fear* (New York: Little, Brown, 1966), *The Call of Service: A Witness to Idealism* (Boston: Houghton Mifflin, 1993), *The Call of Stories* (Boston:

Houghton Mifflin, 1989); Elie Wiesel, *Night* (New York: Bantam, 1960) and *Dawn* (New York: Bantam, 1982); Clifford Geertz, *The Interpretation of Cultures* (New York: Basic Books, 1973); Jerome Bruner, *The Culture of Education* (Cambridge, Mass.: Harvard University Press, 1996); John William Miller, *The Midworld of Symbols and Functioning Objects* (New York: W. W. Norton, 1982); Lee Smolin, *The Life of the Cosmos* (London: Oxford University Press, 1997); and Laurence Shames, *The Hunger for More: Searching for Values in an Age of Greed* (New York: Times Books, 1989).

ACKNOWLEDGMENTS

I would never have seen this book through without the unswerving support and encouragement of my wife Cecilia, *mi compañera del alma*. When times were particularly bleak, Cecilia inspired me to keep moving in the direction of my dreams. The writer Clay Morgan's thoughtful comments on my work in progress at an early stage were critical in helping steer it in the right direction. Alane Mason, my editor at Norton, inspired me not just to write the book I knew I was capable of writing but to write the book I didn't realize I had it in me to write. Collaborating with her has been the most rewarding experience of my writing life. Stefanie Diaz, assistant to Alane Mason, read and commented on my manuscript at a critical point and helped prompt me to make invaluable revisions.

Many others deserve thanks and praise: my mom, Margaret Ann P. Phillips, who continually encouraged me and never doubted I'd eventually succeed; Robert Coles, James Agee Professor of Social Ethics and professor of psychiatry and medical humanities at Harvard University; Morris Dees, founder and executive director of the Southern Poverty Law Center; Gordon Haist, professor of philosophy at the University of South Carolina and a dear friend who provided much-needed understanding and guidance at a particularly critical crossroads; Felicia Eth, my agent for this book; Bill Pennington, professor of philosophy at Delta State University (DSU); Henry Outlaw, chairman of the department of physical sciences at DSU, and John Thornell, graduate dean at DSU, who in a serendipitous encounter helped set my life on a dramatically new course; Carla Narrett, graduate dean at Montclair State University (MSU), who singlehandedly helped ensure that I could continue to pursue my aspirations as a philosopher; Nick Sexton, who gave me my first book by Walter Kaufmann; Alex Phillips, my dad; John Esterle; Shelley Gabriel; the late Alex Haley, a beloved friend who for years exhorted me to write a book; the late Marc Sautet; Rebecca Pitner and Casey Pitner; Joey and Susannah Fox; John Rice Irwin; Patty Canonico; Mary Canonico; the late Steve Canonico; Jake Baer, longtime buddy; James F. Phillips, my uncle; Steve Marchetti; Pat McGee, cherished and true-blue friend; Tom McGee, my pal who always kept the faith; Marlene Carter; Bill Hayes; David Williams; Carlos Loddo; Rob Horn and Elizabeth Kraft; Andrew Burton; Jim Morgan; Mike D'Orso; Jillian Hershberger; the late Melissa Wescott; Scott McCord; Barbara "Auntie Bubbles" Beloff; Cecilia Espinosa; Patty Pyott; Yvonne Espinosa; Josh Glenn; Jacob Needleman, professor of philosophy at San Francisco State University; Ann Margaret Sharp; Philip Guin; Nick DeMatt, who is like family; Walter Anderson of Parade Publications, a cherished mentor; my brother Mike Phillips; and Mat Lipman, exemplary human being and teacher, and unswerving supporter.

And I want to thank all the many, many people who have enriched my life beyond measure by seeking Socrates with me.